TRUE CRIME CASE HISTORIES

VOLUME 11

JASON NEAL

IDIGITAL GROUP

Cover images of:

Elliot Rodger: (top-left)

Jade Janks: (top-right)

Kraig Kahler: (bottom-left)

Riley Gaul: (bottom-right)

More books by Jason Neal

Looking for more?? I am constantly adding new volumes of True Crime Case Histories. The series **can be read in any order,** and all books are available in paperback, hardcover, and audiobook.

Check out the complete series at:

https://amazon.com/author/jason-neal

All Jason Neal books are also available in **AudioBook format at Audible.com.** Enjoy a **Free Audiobook** when you signup for a 30-Day trial using this link:

https://geni.us/AudibleTrueCrime

FREE BONUS EBOOK FOR MY READERS

As my way of saying "Thank you" for downloading, I'm giving away a FREE True Crime e-book I think you'll enjoy.

https://TrueCrimeCaseHistories.com

Just visit the link above to let me know where to send your free book!

INTRODUCTION

If you've read any of my other books, you already know that I begin each one with a brief cautionary statement. True crime can be hard to handle. It's not like watching a crime drama on television. These stories are true, and they have deeply affected real people. This book, like the others in my True Crime Case Histories series, delves into the souls of some of the most evil people the world has ever seen. Pure evil.

True crime is not for everyone. However, there is a small subset of us that, for some reason or another, finds themselves drawn to true crime stories. Perhaps it's a desire for truth and justice, an obsession with understanding the criminal mind, or just curiosity about how the cases were solved. For me, it's the latter. I've been obsessed with forensic science since I first learned the phrase.

To bring you these stories, I've spent hours of research with my nose buried in old newspapers, court documents, police reports, and firsthand accounts. Although some of the details might be disturbing, I've included them not to shock but to give readers a better understanding of the criminal mind. Even if we never learn what drives these diabolical monsters, their depravity will keep us turning pages.

Having said that, if shocking details disturb you easily, this book might not be for you. However, if you're up for it, let's dive in together to uncover the chilling truth.

————

True Crime Case Histories Volume 11 brings to light twelve new stories spanning the past fifty years, exposing the dark realities of human behavior. Within the pages of this book, you'll discover a collection of captivating narratives. Among them, you'll read about a husband who spirals into madness when he learns of his wife's same-sex love affair. With his once ironclad control over his wife shattered, he resorts to unspeakable acts to show his twisted view of power.

Another story highlights the disturbing descent of a troubled young man with psychological issues, deep-seated resentment, and misogynistic and racist beliefs who carried out a horrific rampage, targeting women and innocent bystanders as a violent expression of his distorted worldview.

You'll read the story of the haunting investigation triggered by the disappearance of an eight-year-old girl, where a cryptic note uncovered by a Sunday School teacher unveils an unimaginable deception.

There's also the tale from a small Ohio town, where the discovery of a lifeless body in a suburban home's basement sets off a complex web of secrets, deceit, and hidden relationships.

You'll find the tale of a successful interior designer who learns that someone she's trusted her entire life has secretly amassed a collection of her intimate photos, prompting her to take drastic measures to ensure he pays the ultimate price for his actions.

In another disturbing tale, you'll learn of a seventeen-year-old boy who derives immense pleasure from the sound of someone else's bones breaking.

Yet another story details the life of a wealthy and privileged British investment banker who, in a cocaine-fueled rage, lured young women to his opulent Hong Kong hi-rise apartment only to brutally torture and kill them while videotaping the mayhem.

…Plus, many more true crime stories.

These twelve unputdownable true crime tales will give you a glimpse into the darker side of humanity that lingers long after you turn the final page.

———

Before you continue, I encourage you to join my mailing list for discounts, updates, and a free e-book. You can sign up for that at

TrueCrimeCaseHistories.com

Additional photos, videos, and documents pertaining to the cases in this volume can be found on the accompanying web page at:

http://TrueCrimeCaseHistories.com/vol11/

Thanks again for reading, and I sincerely hope you gain some insight from this volume of True Crime Case Histories.

- Jason Neal

CHAPTER 1
THE SUNDAY SCHOOL TEACHER

T racy, California, a charming city in the San Joaquin Valley, had a lot to offer. It had a lively atmosphere, plenty of recreational activities, and a variety of community events, making it an attractive place to live. People were drawn to Tracy not only for its beautiful parks and trails but also its affordable housing options and numerous amenities. It was a desirable haven for residents of northern California.

But on March 27, 2009, Tracy's peaceful image changed forever. Sandra Cantu, an adorable eight-year-old, skipped happily across the street outside her home and was never seen again. Sandra lived in Orchard Estates Mobile Home Park with her mother, Maria Chavez, her grandparents, and three older siblings. Her life had been simple and happy, filled with the laughter and joy of childhood.

———

It was an ordinary Friday for Sandra, a hardworking second-grader attending Melville S. Jacobson Elementary School. After school, she returned home, and like any other kid, she ventured outside to play with a friend, wandering through the peaceful neighborhood streets. She returned home shortly afterward but soon wandered off again to see another friend, promising her mother she'd be home for dinner.

As dinnertime approached, Sandra's mother grew concerned when she hadn't arrived home. Still, mostly unworried, she asked her son to walk through the neighborhood to find her. Most likely, she was at the neighborhood park just around the corner. But when Sandra's brother returned without her, Maria's heart sank. Panic set in when the boy said he'd looked everywhere. With dinner still on the table, Maria and her other children frantically searched the neighborhood, but fear took hold as the evening grew darker. Sandra had disappeared.

At 7:53 p.m., Maria Chavez mustered the courage to call the authorities and report Sandra Cantu missing. Her voice trembled with anguish as she pleaded for help. The news spread as the city held its breath. Echoes of a distraught mother's cries resonated throughout the town of Tracy.

A sense of urgency drove the police to act quickly. Adrenaline and a strong desire for Sandra's safe return propelled them into action, yet they braced themselves for the grim possibility that their search might reveal a nightmarish truth.

Desperate and distraught, Maria recounted the day's events to detectives. She emphasized that it had been just another typical day, highlighting the improbability of Sandra willingly leaving the safety of the mobile home park. The weight of the situation hung heavy, casting an invisible shadow over the close-knit community.

Without hesitation, the police enlisted the help of trained search dogs to track the scent of the missing child. The dogs darted through the maze of trailers, their paws racing against time, but the night yielded no breakthroughs. Frustration replaced hope as darkness thwarted their efforts.

Undeterred, the search intensified over the weekend of March 28 and 29. A symphony of resources came together, with equestrian teams, ATVs, and helicopters from the California Highway Patrol joining the effort. Search crews scoured every inch of the surrounding areas near her home, but there was no sign of Sandra. She had just vanished.

As days blurred together, the police faced a daunting challenge. They expanded their search, conducting interviews with residents of the trailer park who had criminal records. However, the sheer number of individuals with such histories overwhelmed the investigation, stretching their resources to the limit.

In their search for answers, the police turned to technology, relying on surveillance cameras as silent witnesses. Positioned to capture the daily activities around Sandra's home, these cameras held the potential to reveal hidden truths. Every frame was meticulously examined, as each second hoped to unravel the mystery.

Sandra's family grappled with their worst fears, haunted by the image of her carefree spirit. In the video footage, her arms swayed above her head as she enthusiastically crossed the quiet street, unaware of the evil lurking nearby. The little girl hadn't a care in the world. In the surveillance footage, her long brown hair fell into her eyes, and she brushed it away to look at something south of her home. She then veered away from her doorstep, heading south, where the camera's view ended. It was the last tangible trace they had of her.

To harness the power of collective knowledge, the police established a dedicated tip line. They implored the public to come forward with any information that could help the investigation. The footage of Sandra's final moments reached national news networks, broadcasting the plea for clues into homes across the country, hoping to trigger memories and uncover buried secrets. Though leads came in, none were helpful, and detectives lost hope with each minute that passed.

As the situation grew graver, the FBI joined the expanding investigation and lent its expertise. The collaboration between local law enforcement and the federal agency brought renewed hope and fresh perspectives. FBI agents meticulously searched the mobile home park, scouring every corner for elusive traces of the missing girl. However, despite their exhaustive efforts, no breakthroughs emerged, leaving the community on the verge of despair.

In an effort to gather leads, a reward of $22,000 was offered for any information leading to Sandra's whereabouts. Again, the public supplied tips, but most served only as a distraction.

As the investigation explored various possibilities, one unsettling path had to be examined. It was not uncommon for a parent involved in a custody battle to take a child, removing them from the familiar world they knew. The police had a duty to investigate whether Sandra's father, engaged in a contentious dispute over child support, had resorted to desperate measures. With conviction in her voice, Maria vouched for her ex-partner's character, affirming that he would never harm Sandra. Regardless of her assurances, the focus of the investigation shifted to examining phone records and verifying alibis until Sandra's father was cleared of suspicion.

Delving deeper into Sandra Cantu's disappearance, FBI profilers worked tirelessly to construct a profile of the potential perpetrator. Their analysis pointed to a chilling yet predictable suspect: a white male, aged between 25 and 40, with a history of sexual assault or involvement in child pornography.

Amidst the fog of uncertainty, a local man emerged as an early suspect. He was a karate teacher who lived in the same trailer park, and he had previously crossed paths with Sandra. Witnesses recalled an incident two years prior when he was seen kissing the young girl on the lips at the community swimming pool when she was only six years old. The FBI, swift in their pursuit of leads, called him in for an interview to explore his connection to Sandra's disappearance.

The karate teacher maintained that the kiss had been innocent, merely playful, and with no sinister intentions. Nonetheless, the authorities thoroughly searched his trailer, hoping to find any evidence linking Sandra to his residence. Their efforts led to a startling discovery: a red substance on the floor. Seizing the potential breakthrough, the substance was sent for analysis. However, to everyone's relief, it didn't match Sandra's DNA. Furthermore, the karate teacher's alibi stood strong, as he was confirmed to have been teaching karate on the other side of town during the hours of Sandra's disappearance. With heavy hearts, the investigators cleared him of any involvement, realizing that the true face of the perpetrator had yet to be revealed.

Desperate for answers, the police dispatched search teams to the city landfills, hoping, but simultaneously not hoping, to find any trace of Sandra's presence. An agonizing search ensued, with the haunting possibility that her life had been tragically cut short and her body discarded amidst the waste. During the search, a small Hello Kitty shirt was discovered, briefly capturing the attention of the investigation team. However, as they examined it, they realized it was the wrong color and size.

An unexpected turn of events unfolded during a community vigil for Sandra Cantu. A neighbor, Melissa Huckaby, overwhelmed with emotions and tears streaming down her face, approached police officers and FBI agents. In her hand was a note she claimed to have found near the mailboxes of the trailer park. Her distress was evident as she struggled to speak through gasps for breath.

———

Melissa Huckaby was a twenty-eight-year-old Sunday school teacher at Clover Road Baptist Church, where her grandfather served as the pastor. She also lived in Orchard Estates Mobile Home Park, and her own daughter had been best friends with Sandra. Their lives were intertwined within the close-knit community.

The note she presented to the authorities carried a chilling message riddled with misspellings: "Cantu locked in stolin suitcase. Thrown in water onn Bacchetti Road and Whitehall Road. - Witness." The words sent shivers down their spines and unsettled the delicate balance between hope and despair.

Investigators, however, found certain aspects of Melissa's account puzzling. It struck them as odd that she claimed to have randomly discovered the note on the ground. No such note had been found earlier, despite exhaustive searches throughout the trailer park. Why was the note found randomly on the ground and not sent directly to the family, police, or media?

Another curious detail puzzled investigators. Why would the perpetrator mention the suitcase being stolen instead of just stating that it was a suitcase? It seemed an unnecessary and unusual distinction, defying logical reasoning. They grappled with the puzzle, attempting to comprehend the intentions behind such specific wording.

The police then conducted a thorough forensic analysis of the note, looking for fingerprints that might lead them to its author. Simultaneously, Melissa Huckaby became a person of interest, prompting investigators to delve deeper into her connection to the case. A cloud of suspicion settled over the Sunday school teacher, thrusting her into the spotlight of scrutiny. But Melissa didn't fit the FBI profile in the slightest bit.

Late that night, detectives sat down with Melissa for an interview, determined to uncover any hidden truths beneath her tearful demeanor. She revealed that her trailer was just eight doors from Sandra's family, and her daughter had shared a close friendship with the missing girl. When asked about her whereabouts on the day Sandra vanished, Melissa told detectives she had been preparing for Sunday school at the church where she worked.

A troubling pattern emerged as the investigation delved deeper into Melissa's life. Detectives discovered she had a history of grappling with mental health challenges, including borderline personality disorder, bipolar disorder, and schiz-ophrenia. Melissa had repeatedly engaged in self-harm, started fires, and subjected others to verbal and psychological attacks, all in desperate attempts to draw attention to herself.

————

Undeterred by the complexities of the case, the police took the note seriously and went to the location it mentioned—a site three miles away from the trailer park. Search and rescue teams braved the challenging terrain of an agricultural manure reservoir, meticulously scouring the area. Dive teams, however, were unable to assist due to the murkiness of the manure-filled pond, which offered zero visibility. Despite their exhaustive efforts, they found no suitcase, no evidence, nor any trace that Sandra had been there.

Detectives then revisited the last remnants of video footage capturing Sandra's final moments near her home. Analyzing the footage frame by frame, they noted that the young girl had been seen walking south down the dead-end street. Only thirteen trailers were south of her home. Among those residing in that direction, only one person had a connection to Sandra—Melissa Huckaby.

Investigators attempted a second interview with Huckaby but discovered she had checked herself into the hospital after swallowing a razor blade. A suicide attempt. Her hospitalization added complexity to the investigation, as authorities needed to consider her mental state.

A cloud of devastation descended upon Tracy, California, as a grim discovery shattered any lingering hope. During a routine draining of an irrigation pond on April 6, authorities stumbled upon a haunting sight—a black and gray Eddie Bauer suitcase, its zipper tied together with a thin, white cord. The weight of apprehension hung in the air as they transported the ominous case to the medical examiner's office, bracing themselves for the truth it concealed.

With trembling hands, they carefully unzipped the suitcase to reveal the lifeless body of Sandra Cantu, crumpled into the fetal position. She still wore her pink Hello Kitty t-shirt and black leggings. The sanctuary of childhood had been viciously violated; her spirit forever extinguished by the unimaginable horrors she had endured.

With the lifeless body of Sandra Cantu uncovered from the suitcase, the medical examiner's office began its meticulous examination of the evidence. The autopsy revealed that Sandra had suffered both physical and sexual abuse. Evidence that she had been sexually abused with a foreign object left no doubt about the torment she had faced.

Toxicology results revealed the presence of Xanax in Sandra's system, indicating that she had been drugged. This discovery added another layer of complexity to the investigation, raising questions about the circumstances surrounding her final hours.

The eerie parallels between the circumstances of Sandra's discovery and the note Melissa Huckaby claimed to have found could not be ignored. However, despite the peculiarities surrounding Melissa's behavior and her history of mental health struggles, authorities, including the FBI, concluded that her actions were likely misguided cries for attention. As a result, the investigation refocused its efforts on identifying and apprehending the person truly responsible for Sandra's tragic fate.

———

Detectives returned to the reservoir and spoke to a couple who lived close to where the suitcase was discovered. When asked if they had noticed anything unusual recently, the couple told the police they had seen a woman with a purple SUV near the irrigation pond.

The woman's vehicle was parked on their property near the intersection of Bacchetti Road and Whitehall Road between 5:30 p.m. and 6 p.m. on the day Sandra went missing. According to the couple, the woman seemed preoccupied and rushed. When they approached her and questioned why she was on their property, she replied, "I just needed to pee real quick."

Drawing upon the couple's testimony, detectives intensified their efforts to uncover the mysterious woman's identity and determine her connection to Sandra's abduction and murder. The description of the woman and her distinctive purple SUV became a focal point for the investigation.

Investigators again scoured surveillance footage from nearby establishments, seeking any glimpses of the purple SUV around the time of Sandra's disappearance. They reviewed hours of video, analyzing intersections and roadways in hopes of catching a crucial lead. Their persistence paid off when a gas station's surveillance camera captured a purple SUV that matched the witnesses' description. The timestamp aligned with the timeline of the couple's encounter, further strengthening this breakthrough's significance.

———

Upon reviewing the video footage from within the trailer park once again, detectives made a significant discovery. At 3:54 p.m. on the day of Sandra's disappearance, they had observed Sandra walking south—toward Melissa's house. However, just eight minutes later, the camera also captured Melissa Huckaby driving a purple SUV, which perfectly matched the description provided by the couple who had seen it near where Sandra's body was eventually discovered. The SUV departed the trailer park approximately twenty minutes later and headed toward the reservoir.

Detectives learned that, just minutes after she drove away from the neighborhood, Huckaby had called the trailer park manager to report that her Eddie Bauer suitcase had been stolen from her trailer.

After eighty-five minutes, another surveillance camera placed outside the church where Huckaby taught Sunday school captured Huckaby's vehicle as it drove away. Another thirty-five minutes later, the footage showed her returning to the church.

During this thirty-minute window, the couple spotted Huckaby and her purple SUV near the irrigation pond.

———

Detectives later discovered that, on the day Sandra disappeared, Melissa sent a peculiar text to Sandra's mother mentioning that something had been stolen around 4 p.m., and it might help with the investigation. Melissa had a suitcase that she wanted to report stolen.

When detectives interviewed Melissa again, she was still in the hospital. She confirmed her story about her stolen suitcase on the day Sandra disappeared and expressed her sorrow upon hearing about Sandra's body being found.

Authorities began to scrutinize Huckaby much more closely. They found it highly suspicious that she, out of everyone in the area, reported losing a suitcase and then coincidentally discovered a note indicating that the same stolen suitcase was used to conceal the child's body.

Melissa Huckaby, held within the hospital ward, became the prime suspect in the chilling saga. Detectives approached her once again, carefully navigating her words and emotions. Despite her feigned sorrow upon learning about Sandra's tragic fate, the detectives knew that a dark secret lurked beneath her remorse.

The mounting evidence against Melissa painted a damning picture of guilt, revealing her malicious intentions. Each discovery brought the detectives closer to uncovering the truth, exposing Melissa's sinister nature, and bringing to light the unspeakable acts she had committed.

———

A search of the church where she worked provided substantial evidence. A window drawstring from her Sunday school classroom had been recently cut. The string matched perfectly with that which bound the suitcase zippers together. Investigators also found isopropyl alcohol in both the church and Sandra's liver. A bloodstained rolling pin—a haunting discovery—sent shivers through the seasoned investigators. Its twisted handle was a silent witness to the unimaginable brutality inflicted on Sandra. The confirmation of Sandra's DNA on the rolling pin sealed Melissa's fate, exposing her as the cold-hearted perpetrator of the unspeakable crimes that had shattered the tranquility of Tracy, California.

Adding to the unraveling of Melissa Huckaby's twisted psyche, investigators found a spiral-bound notebook in her trailer that bore the chilling title, "Cute, But Psycho - Things Will Even Out." The imprints on its remaining pages confirmed that she had written the note.

While investigating Melissa's online activities, detectives discovered a disturbing digital trail. They came across an article she had read about the deliberate murder of a child who was placed in a suitcase and submerged in water. The revelation exposed the premeditated nature of the crime and established a clear connection between Melissa's fascination with such horrifying acts and the tragic fate that befell Sandra.

Hidden in her SUV, detectives found a sticky note that, under the glow of an alternative light source, revealed three words: Bacchetti, Whitehall, and Water. Every little piece of evidence further cemented her guilt.

———

Melissa Huckaby appeared calm and provided no explanation when she was brought in for questioning one final time. However, when confronted with the evidence against her after nearly four hours of interrogation, she provided an answer. She claimed that she and Sandra had been playing a game of hide and seek. According to Melissa, Sandra hid in the suitcase, but Melissa forgot about her, and tragically, Sandra accidentally suffocated. However, the mountain of evidence contradicted Melissa's story, as she had no explanation for why the girl was drugged and sexually assaulted with a rolling pin, nor why the suitcase was zipped and tied shut.

On April 10, 2009, Melissa Huckaby was arrested and charged with the sexual assault, kidnapping, and murder of Sandra Cantu. She also faced charges of drugging a seven-year-old and an unrelated charge of drugging a thirty-seven-year-old man.

The trial began a year later, but midway through the trial, Melissa was offered a plea deal. As part of the agreement, the drugging charges were dropped, and Melissa pleaded guilty to first-degree murder in order to avoid the death penalty.

Melissa Huckaby was sentenced to life in prison without the possibility of parole. During sentencing, she expressed her struggle to comprehend why she committed such acts—a question that would haunt her for the rest of her life. The prosecutor speculated that Melissa had killed Sandra solely to draw attention to herself.

CHAPTER 2
ROOM 3109

Helen and Graham Jutting lived just a stone's throw away from the bustling city of London, UK, in the historic Foxwarren Cottage. The home was given a Grade Two listing, as it inspired Toad Hall, the fabled home of Mr. Toad from the classic children's novel, "The Wind and The Willows."

While Helen ran an American-style milkshake bar in the nearby town of Woking, Graham was an engineer working for a local company who had a deep love of vintage motorcycles. They successfully accumulated a modest fortune for their family by banding together in their entrepreneurial spirit.

In 1985, a year after they were married, the Juttings welcomed their first son into the family. They were so thrilled that they named him Rurik, after the renowned Russian dynasty that had flourished since its establishment in 862 AD. The name itself held profound significance, as it meant "great one" when translated from Russian.

As a prosperous couple living in London, Graham and Helen spared no effort in making sure Rurik would enjoy the finest things life had to offer. From the onset of his early years, Rurik's mother showered him with unwavering assurance of his exceptional nature. He was repeatedly told that he possessed remarkable gifts and talents, setting him apart from his peers. The constant reinforcement gave Rurik a deep-seated conviction of his superiority, instilling in him an overwhelming sense of self-importance.

During his time in primary school, Rurik's teachers regarded him as an eccentric boy who failed to garner much popularity among his classmates. However, as he entered his early teenage years, he gained admission to Winchester College, a prestigious private school. To Rurik's dismay, the school didn't meet his expectations. He found himself disappointed, harboring resentment for ranking sixth in the scholarship selection rather than being chosen first. Additionally, he found his mother's apparent surprise and delight over his exam results to be deeply offensive. After all, she had spent his entire life assuring him of his superiority over other children, leading him to believe that exceptional achievements were his norm.

At sixteen, Rurik went through the trauma of witnessing his father slit his own wrists in a suicide attempt. Luckily, his father lived after Rurik rushed him to the hospital. Two years later, however, Rurik confided to his psychiatrist that he, too, was having suicidal thoughts. He admitted to his psychiatrist that a boy at his school had sexually assaulted him, and he was troubled by his parents' discussions of divorce.

Despite the challenges he faced, Rurik showed remarkable resilience and perseverance. Following his graduation, he was admitted to Peterhouse College at Cambridge University, where he focused his studies on history and law.

Rurik excelled in the field of history, graduating with first-class honors—a testament to his intellectual capabilities. However, upon discovering that he had received second-class honors in law, Rurik reacted angrily. His narcissistic personality traits, nurtured by a life of privilege, hindered his ability to accept criticism or anything less than perfection. Even though second-class honors were still a commendable accomplishment by any standard, Rurik vehemently contested the grade because of his unwavering desire for approval.

Following his graduation, Rurik Jutting secured a position at Barclays Bank in Canary Wharf, the prominent financial hub of London. However, it didn't take long for Rurik's talents to catch the attention of Bank of America Merrill Lynch, which recognized his ambition and potential. The tempting offer presented to him was simply irresistible, prompting him to make a significant career move.

Rurik took on his new role at Bank of America Merrill Lynch, where he was given the responsibility of developing intricate tax products for the firm. This position came with a substantial salary of £270,000 ($334,705) per year, reflecting the recognition of his skills and the value he brought to the company.

———

Rurik's romantic journey had been fraught with difficulties. While working at Barclays Bank, he fell in love with a colleague named Sarah Butts. However, shortly after they began dating, Sarah was assigned a one-year position in New

York. When she returned to London, she broke the news to Rurik that she had fallen in love with another man, leaving Rurik heartbroken and angry.

Rurik's resentment toward Sarah grew to the point that she became fearful of him and quickly moved back to New York to distance herself from the explosive situation. Rurik found himself unable to get over the hurt the affair had caused.

With his lifetime of perceived entitlement and newly-found wealth, Rurik began experimenting with drugs and hiring sex workers. The more drugs he consumed, the more his sexual obsessions grew. By the time he was twenty-four, his sexual needs had grown sadistic and violent. He began fantasizing about rape, torture, and kidnapping. While having sex with prostitutes, he developed the habit of removing his condom without letting the girl know. Exchanging sexual services for money was not a crime in the United Kingdom, but removing his condom without consent carried a charge of rape. The sex workers, however, refused to bring charges against him.

In 2012, auditors began investigating Bank of America Merrill Lynch concerning potential regulatory violations related to their tax activities in Luxembourg—the same division where Jutting had been working. The executives within the company perceived Rurik's conduct and negligent approach to work as a significant risk to the organization's reputation and compliance. To address the ongoing investigation and avoid terminating him, he was transferred to the Hong Kong office in 2013.

Rurik became the Vice President and Head of Structured Equity Finance in Hong Kong. This transfer allowed the company to prevent potential negative consequences from the investigation while allowing Rurik to continue his employment.

But before his transfer to Hong Kong, Jutting had already spiraled into a deep depression. He often cried at work, snorted cocaine during the day, and needed almost an entire bottle of vodka each night to get to sleep. Just before he boarded his flight to Hong Kong, Rurik filled a balloon with cocaine and slid it into his rectum. It would be enough to get him by until he found a new dealer in Hong Kong.

Once settled in Hong Kong, Rurik secured a rental flat in the prestigious J Residence, a renowned luxury development in Wanchai. His residence, room 3109, offered an impressive location just a short distance from the rooftop amenities like the swimming pool, bar, and garden, granting him breath-taking views of the vibrant Hong Kong skyline.

But Rurik saw his move to Hong Kong as a step down in his career, which made him even more unhappy; this made him act more and more erratic. His new managers found him to be one of the most unpredictable and challenging employees they had ever encountered.

In his personal life, Rurik embraced his newfound surround-ings by immersing himself in the company of beautiful, local women. He showcased his glamorous lifestyle through social media updates and Facebook posts. He soon fell in love with a woman named Aryan Guarin, who also went by the name Yani. From the outside, their relationship looked very passionate. Rurik's behavior changed in a disturbing way, however, when he became obsessed with orgies and drug-fueled parties with multiple partners. This irresponsible behavior went hand in hand with his propensity for exces-sive spending, which ultimately led him to give up on his previous passions and interests. Eventually, their relationship crumbled under the weight of Rurik's erratic behavior.

Following the breakup, Rurik became isolated and retreated from any social interaction. His grueling sixteen-hour workdays wore on him, and he sought solace in a self-destructive cycle of substance abuse, encounters with sex workers, and excessive alcohol consumption. He spent the majority of his free time in his own apartment, spending hours indulging in alcohol and video games. A deep sense of hopelessness and nihilism consumed him, and his mental state degraded more and more.

Those still connected to him watched as Rurik's demeanor went over the edge. He became increasingly aggressive, took more significant risks without regard for consequences, and projected an aloof and detached attitude. Concerns grew among his friends as they watched the gradual unraveling of his sanity.

By 2014, Rurik Jutting had completely succumbed to the destructive forces that had taken control of his life, falling into a dark abyss of addiction and aberrant behavior. He found himself spending his days in isolation and grappling with the grip of his addictions. Cocaine had become his constant companion, and he engaged in prolonged binges that lasted for days. His addiction had grown so powerful that it led him to miss an important work meeting in London. In a desperate attempt to cover his tracks, he fabricated an outrageous lie, claiming to have contracted HIV.

————

By mid-October 2014, Rurik had become increasingly detached from his professional obligations and hadn't been to work for almost two weeks. He spent his days and nights in his apartment watching violent porn, drinking, and doing drugs. Yet, no matter how much he indulged, nothing seemed to satisfy his needs. Filled with desperation and a longing for new experiences, he turned to Grindr, a gay hookup app, in a futile attempt to find satisfaction and connection with other men. However, every encounter left him empty and disappointed, further fueling his sense of despair.

———

A few short weeks later, Jutting exploited Sumarti "Alice" Ningsih, who was only nineteen years old at the time. Desperate for money, she had just arrived in Hong Kong from Indonesia on a tourist visa, and the two had met at a nearby hotel. The promise of money enticed Alice to Jutting's apartment, but instead she became the victim of Jutting's violent, sexual obsessions. Alice begged him to stop, but he ignored her pleas. Eventually, he agreed to let her go, but on October 25, 2014, he lured her again with an exorbitant sum of money and false promises that nothing crazy would happen. She reluctantly followed him to his apartment in room 3109, never imagining the evil fate ahead.

Alice walked into the apartment, unaware of the horror that awaited her. Jutting's demented cravings had to be fed, and he used tools of torture—including pliers, sex toys, his belt, and even his fists—to subdue her. Capturing every horrific moment on his cellphone camera, the abuse continued for two days while Jutting snorted cocaine as if it were fuel for his monstrous acts.

Finally, on the third day, Jutting dragged Alice to the bathroom, forcing her to kneel before the toilet and lick it clean.

He then produced a knife and, without hesitation, slashed her throat with a single stroke. The wound proved insufficient to take her life, so he dragged her into the shower to finish what he had started, slicing her throat and nearly decapitating her.

Afterward, Jutting recorded videos describing the atrocity he committed in gruesome detail, all the while snorting cocaine, drinking vodka, and contemplating his life choices. He then wrapped her body in bath towels, crumpled her into the fetal position, and forced it into a large suitcase, which he rolled out the sliding door and onto the balcony.

On October 31st, he ventured out to a hardware store, where he bought sandpaper, nails, and a blowtorch. Using his iPhone, he recorded videos showing each torture device and his plans to use them on future victims.

That night, the unsuspecting Jesse Lorena Ruri met with Jutting at the New Makati Pub and Disco. Jesse, an Indonesian immigrant who had lived in Hong Kong for eight years, worked as a domestic helper and part-time DJ in Hong Kong's red-light district. Little did she know that this would be her last outing in Hong Kong. In a few hours, she'd lie lifeless in a pool of blood on his sofa.

Leaving for his apartment, an uncomfortable chill ran up Jesse's spine as they entered. A disgusting smell filled the air as they stepped further into the apartment. She messaged a friend, "Something smells really bad. I want to get out of here."

A sickening sensation suddenly overwhelmed her when she saw a ball gag near the couch. Instinctively, Jesse screamed out loud, only to find a sharp blade held against her throat as Jutting warned her not to scream. But it was too late—a

fearful whimper escaped her lips while she frantically struggled to free herself. With one swift movement of his arm, he
slid the blade across her neck and watched as the life slowly
drained out of her. She didn't give him the opportunity to
use his planned torture tools.

———

Jutting's apartment felt like a prison, with two dead bodies
and the knowledge of what he had done weighing on him.
He reached for another line of cocaine and took a long swig
from his bottle of bourbon as he stepped out onto the
balcony. He could end it all right now if he just jumped—but
something held him back. Instead, he changed the voicemail
message on his work phone,

> "I'm out of the office. Indefinitely. For urgent
> inquiries, or indeed any inquiries, please contact
> someone who is not an insane psychopath. For
> escalation, please contact God, though I suspect
> the devil will have custody. ...That last line only
> really worked if I had followed through."

He then posted on Facebook,

> "Stepping back from the ledge. Burden lifted. A
> new journey begins. Scared and anxious, but
> also excited. The first step is always the hardest."

Jutting paced around his living room, the phone shaking in
his hand as he dialed his boss. "I'm in a lot of trouble. You
need to do something about the reputation of the bank," he
croaked out, pulling the phone away from his ear and staring
at the walls that seemed to close in on him. A few moments

later, Jutting hung up, and he felt a sense of panic wash over him. The seconds ticked by like hours until 3:42 a.m., when desperation got the better of him. He again picked up the phone and dialed the police. He babbled about "something happening" in his apartment, and he then made two more desperate calls to the police, begging them to arrive sooner.

Two officers cautiously arrived at the scene. They opened the front door to find Jesse's blood-soaked, naked body sprawled across the living room floor, her pale neck and buttock punctured with deep knife wounds. A twelve-inch blade and a blood-stained sex toy lay beside her body, while a pile of twenty-six small bags of cocaine rested nearby. Jutting stood in blood-soaked shoes, his hands and clothes splattered in dried crimson, muttering incoherent words under his breath. As the police stepped closer, they heard a faint gurgle coming from Jesse. She was still alive. The paramedics worked swiftly to get her to the hospital, but it was too late; when they arrived, she had already died.

———

Crime scene investigators scoured the scene, took photographs, and collected evidence that would forensically reveal the nature of her death. It took eight hours before they followed the trail of blood and made their way to the balcony, where they found a large black suitcase with a broken lock containing Alice Ningsih's body. Her head was partially decapitated, and her legs and arms were still bound with rope.

———

As police took 29-year-old Rurik Jutting into custody, they were horrified to hear his confession. In a calm and assertive voice, he told detectives he wished he could have tortured Alice much more before killing her.

Jutting confessed to his brutal torture, telling detectives,

> "I've never seen anyone that scared. She voluntarily ate feces out of the toilet, and then she smiled at me afterward. I urinated into her mouth. She threw up, and I made her eat her own vomit. I made her take drugs. I beat her pussy so badly she bled from her labia."

On his iPhone, investigators found over 2,000 photos and dozens of videos. Over 1,000 images were sexual, some showing him posing with the partially severed head of Alice. He had recorded over four hours of himself rambling into the camera about his life and the crimes he had committed. He spoke of the pleasure he enjoyed from torturing the girls, with Jesse's lifeless body visible in the background.

> "My name is Rurik Jutting. About five minutes ago, I just killed and murdered this woman here. It's Monday night. I've held her captive since early Saturday. I feel a bit sad because she was a good person, but I don't really feel guilty. My hand is still shaking, and I feel sick, but I don't feel guilty. But clearly, I feel something. I can't describe what it means. I don't recognize myself. I've basically been lying on the sofa for the whole week. The things I get up for are coke, alcohol, and food. And I've had a lot of Pizza

Express lasagna. I'm waiting to be kicked out by the police."

The videos he recorded were confessions in and of themselves. In one, he taunted Alice in a relaxed tone,

> "Do not move. That's a good girl. Do you like the fucking fist?" he said as he forced his closed fist into her vagina. "Good girl. See, it's not that bad. It's better than being beaten, right?"

He then went on, threatening to cut off her nipples.

> "This doesn't really hurt, does it? You deserve some water, don't you? Just one more before some water."

In yet another video, he discussed a sadistic fantasy he had of kidnapping three teenage girls from Wycombe Abbey boarding school in northwest London.

> "They would be, say, fifteen years old, and I would basically turn these three girls into my sex slaves. It would be good to psychologically play them off against each other."

In another video, he urinated into a beer glass and expressed his fears of being sent to a Hong Kong prison. He bragged about his high salary but referred to himself as a "part-time rapist and murderer."

———

Rurik Jutting boldly declared his guilt in two horrific murders yet submitted a plea of not guilty on the grounds of diminished responsibility. He did, however, accept the blame for manslaughter. The judge brought in four psychiatrists to evaluate Rurik's mental state. They all concurred that he had a narcissistic personality disorder, though he was still capable of being held accountable for his actions.

At the trial, Rurik's harrowing testimony took the jury through the grotesque horrors of his three-day torture session. He explained how he had lured Alice into his hotel room with an offer of 10,000 Hong Kong dollars for her company. What unfolded was an unspeakable nightmare of flesh-tearing tools, each used to inflict unimaginable physical suffering on her in a marathon of cruel depravity.

On October 31st, at 12:51 PM, a surveillance camera captured Rurik leaving his apartment shortly after killing Alice. He returned an hour later with bags containing a blowtorch, hammer, nails, pliers, and sandpaper purchased from a nearby hardware store. After putting his bags down, he went to the pub just around the corner. There, he found Jesse. They left for his apartment in the early morning hours, and within an hour and a half of arriving, Jesse was dead.

———

The defense's experts presented a clinical assessment of Rurik Jutting's psychological state, revealing details of his exceptional intelligence (a tested IQ of 137) and the diagnoses that had gone unseen for years. They confirmed that Jutting was struggling with four severe disorders that had manifested in murderous behavior just weeks before he took the lives of two innocent women:

Narcissistic personality disorder - an ailment that often leads to an inflated sense of self-importance and a lack of empathy toward others. The defense argued that his narcissism had been evident in Jutting at an early age.

Sexual sadism disorder - which can cause an individual to derive pleasure from causing pain and suffering to others.

Cocaine and alcohol use disorders - dangerous addictions that can lead to erratic and violent behavior.

Rurik's guilt seemed inevitable as the jury heard the overwhelming evidence against him: surveillance footage, the cold corpses of his victims, incriminating receipts, a slew of menacing emails, over two thousand damning photos, and four hours of unsettling confession videos. As if it weren't enough for them to hear the details of Jutting's sadistic crimes, they were shown a twenty-minute clip depicting a shirtless Rurik, overweight and ranting wildly. At the same time, poor Alice lay lifeless near the toilet—an image that would remain permanently branded in the jury's mind forever.

> "I just killed someone—the first person I ever killed. I cut her throat in the bathroom. To be precise, I cut her throat while she was bending over, licking the dirty toilet bowl. I treated her as a non-person, a sex object. And that turned me on."

The judge, Mr. Justice Michael Stuart Moore, scolded Rurik, calling him a heinous man consumed by the darkness of his depraved actions spurred on by cocaine and alcohol.

The jury's decision was unanimous. Rurik Jutting was found guilty of murder on November 8th, 2016. As the verdict was read, Rurik had no reaction. His icy calm clashed sharply with the cries of those around him. At sentencing, Jutting was handed two consecutive life sentences.

The trial of their son weighed heavily on his parents. On the eve of the court case, Helen and Graham Jutting ended their thirty-two-year marriage in divorce.

CHAPTER 3
HIDDEN BETRAYAL

The wealthy enclave of Solana Beach is tucked away in the northernmost parts of San Diego, and Jade Janks called it home. Jade was a skilled interior designer who, in 2018, started her own business under the name Jade Janks Design. Within a relatively short period, she amassed an impressive net worth of 15 million dollars.

But Jade wasn't alone on her path to success. Born to Jenny and Steve Janks on October 14, 1983, she grew up amid her father's construction business, which provided stability for the family. Unfortunately, her parents' marriage ended when she was just ten years old. Despite the divorce, Jade maintained a close relationship with her father while living primarily with her mother.

By 1995, Jade's mother, Jenny, had found love once again and married a man named Tom Merriman. Jade welcomed her half-brother, Cash, into the family. Although they weren't related through blood, their sibling bond was strong.

The family experienced their fair share of ups and downs. Jenny and Tom's marriage faced repeated challenges, resulting in multiple divorces. They first divorced in 2002. They then remarried, only to get divorced again in 2006. They repeated the process yet again before divorcing for a final time in 2008. Despite their disagreements, they kept their relationship civil and preserved the family's connections.

Working closely with her father's construction company, Jade's interests shifted as she entered adulthood, and she became more interested in interior design. After high school, she pursued her passion at San Diego's Misa College while still working alongside her father. With youth, ambition, and beauty on her side, Jade sought a life of luxury and indulgence. She yearned for extravagant experiences, from boat trips to designer clothing and fine dining.

Although Jade worked hard toward her professional path, her family remained important. She kept close ties with her mother, father, and stepfather, Tom. Although divorced from her mother, Tom played a significant role in Jade's life and provided unwavering support as she grew her career. However, as time passed, their roles reversed; she became his caregiver in his later years while he battled alcoholism and an addiction to sleeping pills.

As the years progressed, Jade's determination propelled her professional growth. With her father's assistance, she made significant strides in the design industry and established her interior design firm, Jade Janks Interiors. Meanwhile, Tom Merriman found his success in opening a non-profit butterfly farm in 2013, seeking to bring beauty to Solana Beach.

———

On the dawn of New Year's Day in 2021, the Solana Beach Police Department basked in a calm atmosphere as the usual chaos of drunken disagreements and minor crimes of New Year's Eve faded away. Unbeknownst to the officers, a chilling event was about to disrupt their peace. Adam Siplyak, a close friend of Jade Janks, arrived at the police station, ready to share a disturbing tale that would unsettle the entire community.

The trouble began on New Year's Eve, around noon, when Jade reached out to Adam to ask for help moving her stepfather, Tom, into his home. Jade explained that she had picked Tom up from the hospital, where he had been recovering from a fall from the week prior. But on the drive home, he guzzled whiskey and took sleeping pills, and now he was passed out; she couldn't get him out of the car.

Although Adam's prior obligations prevented him from extending a helping hand to Jade in her moment of need, he resolved to make amends by surprising her later that evening. With a heart full of good intentions, he arrived at Tom's residence around 7 p.m., unaware of the ominous turn that awaited him.

When he arrived at the house, Adam immediately sensed that something was wrong. It was an unsettling feeling that gnawed at him. His attention was drawn to Jade's parked car, with a large, unmoving figure slumped in the back seat.

Despite Jade's attempts to calm him and provide an explanation, Adam remained resolute in his decision to distance himself from the situation. Without hesitation, he promptly reported his troubling findings to the authorities, his voice quivering with fear and apprehension.

Adam's alarming account prompted officers to go to Tom Merriman's home for a welfare check. However, they found an empty SUV in the driveway with a large pile of debris adjacent to it. Although the pile of trash seemed out of place, it could easily have been from a house cleanup or a remodeling job. The rest of the scene, however, appeared deceptively normal. Knocking on the front door of Tom's home, their calls echoed into silence. The officers peered through the windows but only saw a meticulously clean interior, showing no signs of trouble.

Reluctant to leave, however, a nagging feeling urged the officers to investigate further. After checking the house, they focused on the pile of discarded trash strewn across the driveway. They carefully searched through the remnants until they came across a mysterious object buried beneath an abandoned cardboard box.

When they moved the cardboard, they uncovered the chilling truth—the unmoving body of Tom Merriman. Upon first glance, the cause of his death wasn't obvious. There were many unanswered questions, and detectives needed to find Jade Janks for answers.

———

Tom's untimely demise sent shockwaves of disbelief and despair through those who knew him. The loving support that he and Jade had shared for decades made the idea of his thirty-seven-year-old stepdaughter as a murder suspect unfathomable. The pieces of this puzzle simply didn't fit together.

For several years leading up to his death, Tom had relied on Jade's unwavering support and care. When he faced his struggles with alcohol, Jade was there, diligently tending to his needs. Through the years, her dedication knew no bounds—transporting him to medical appointments, ensuring his medication was obtained, and maintaining his residence in his absence. One week before his death, Tom had been hospitalized following a fall. Jade regularly visited him in the hospital, watched over his home, and tended to his every need.

But during Tom's latest hospital stay, Jade made a horrifying discovery that would scar her soul and leave her with an unrelenting sense of violation. Jade was alone, cleaning Tom's home, when she inadvertently nudged his computer's mouse. She watched as the screensaver flickered to life. There on the screen was a photo of a female breast with a familiar beauty mark. It was unmistakably her breast.

Shocked, she explored the file folders of his computer and uncovered a collection of over a hundred photos of herself. Each photo was meticulously categorized and organized by her body parts. It sickened her. Several images were taken over a decade earlier, when Jade was only sixteen.

To her horror, she realized these were her images—intimate snapshots she had once captured and shared with past romantic partners. They were personal moments meant to be private memories that somehow found their way into the possession of her stepfather. The revelation struck her with a profound sense of violation and unease.

The mystery deepened as she remained clueless about how her intimate images ended up on Tom's computer. However, the chilling truth got worse. She discovered another collection of photos secretly taken without her knowledge or consent, capturing her most private moments in her bathroom and bedroom. Each image she found was a haunting reminder of the violation she had unknowingly endured, intensifying the sense of betrayal and intrusion.

Jade's discovery left her reeling in unimaginable horror. The realization that a figure of paternal authority had preyed upon her for countless years struck her at the very core of her being. She was shattered.

Jade was faced with many choices about how to handle the betrayal. The direction she chose, however, was one that most in her position would not even consider. In her shattered state, her answer to this nightmarish revelation was to seek vengeance through murder—an act that seemed all too easy, given Tom's struggle with substance abuse. With calculated precision, Jade devised a plan to make Tom's death appear accidental, believing she could elude justice.

However, Jade made a critical error in her desperate bid to cover her tracks—she involved others. Dozens of text messages flew between her and Adam Roach, whom she referred to as her "fixer." Roach was a personal security expert she had enlisted to aid in concealing her vicious act.

In her text messages to Roach, she explained her murderous actions in great detail and requested further help. Some of the messages included:

> "I just dosed the hell out of him. Stopping for whiskey then at Dixieland to stall. LMK,"

> "He's waking up... I really don't want to be the one to do this."

> "I'm about to club him on the head as he's waking up."

"I'm not strong enough. He's very aware now and I'm on my own."

"I can't carry him alone. And I can't keep a kicking body in my trunk."

Yet the gravity of her intentions was too much for her accomplice, and he withdrew from the plan at the eleventh hour, leaving Jade in a panic. Then she turned to her friend, Adam Siplyak, for support, hoping he would become an ally in her darkest hour.

When Adam Siplyak arrived, Jade recounted the tale of Tom collapsing in her car after a lethal cocktail of whiskey and sleeping pills. Her voice trembled with sorrow and rage as she painted a picture of a tragic accident, her words a desperate attempt to justify the unforgivable.

But in a moment of vulnerability, Jade couldn't help but tell Adam the gruesome truth. Her voice cracked as she told him what she had uncovered on Tom's computer—a truth that shattered her world and destroyed her perception of him. Tears streamed down Jade's face as she implored Adam, her voice filled with desperation, to aid her in covering up the murder. She begged for his understanding, her words laced with a toxic blend of anger and grief. In her distorted reality, justice could only be served through her own hands, and she saw no other way to find solace than to ensure Tom's secrets remained buried forever.

Adam stood there, his own emotions swirling in a tumultuous storm. He saw the torment etched on Jade's face, the weight of her actions threatening to consume her. A battle raged within him, torn between his loyalty to a friend and the horrifying realization of the depths to which she had sunk. There was a feeling of dread in the air, as if their relationship had been torn apart forever.

Finally, with a heavy sigh, Adam found the strength to utter the words that would forever alter the trajectory of their lives. "No, Jade," he whispered, his voice filled with anguish and resolve.

Jade's heart pounded in her chest, the weight of her secret threatening to crush her. She knew that time was of the essence and that every passing moment increased the risk of discovery. With a surge of panicked energy, she hastily dragged Tom's body out of the car and deposited it in the front driveway, covering it beneath a layer of discarded trash. In her mind, this makeshift disguise hoped to buy her precious time—a chance to strategize and perhaps find a new fixer, who could help erase the traces of her dark deed.

———

Following her arrest, Jade maintained a composed demeanor and cooperated fully with the authorities as they conducted searches at Tom's residence, then later at her own. With substantial wealth at her disposal, she spared no expense in securing the services of top-notch attorneys. She even managed to post her bail, set at a staggering one million dollars. However, these privileges came with restrictions. Jade had to move in with her mother, was limited to a radius of seven miles from her home, and was constantly monitored through a mandatory GPS tracker.

Jade's trial began on December 21st, 2022, granting her two years of freedom before facing a court judgment. Throughout the courtroom drama, Jade's defense vehemently maintained her innocence. They argued that the evidence presented against her was purely circumstantial and that the text messages, which had been used to incriminate her, could be interpreted in various ways when viewed in context.

The prosecution presented a compelling case in response, asserting that Jade had drugged Tom before suffocating him with a plastic bag. Toxicology reports revealed that Tom's cause of death was an overdose of Zolpidem, commonly known as Ambien, a potent sleeping pill.

Jade's defense seized upon this information, presenting it as evidence that Tom's death resulted from a self-inflicted overdose rather than murder. This explanation seemed entirely plausible, given his struggles with alcohol and medication abuse.

The prosecution's case, however, was strengthened by a series of suspicious items discovered inside Jade's car, including red rope, pillowcases, a makeshift rope crafted from three tied-together hand towels, and a receipt for these items from Dixieland, a hardware supply store referenced in the incriminating text messages she exchanged with her fixer.

During her tearful testimony on the witness stand, Jade recounted her emotional state upon discovering her nude images on Tom's computer, unwittingly solidifying a motive for the alleged murder.

Prosecutor Jorge Del Portillo pointed out that not only was Jade motivated by the images she found on Tom's computer, but the items in her car showed that the murder was premeditated.

She also had the opportunity because she was the one who picked Tom up from the hospital, and her confession was clear in the text message that said, "I just dosed the hell out of him."

With the wealth of evidence—including the incriminating items in her car, witness testimonies from Adam Siplyak and her fixer, Adam Roach, and the glaring text messages that served as a damning confession—the jury found her guilty of drugging and strangling her former stepfather after just one day of deliberation.

On Monday, March 6, 2023, Jade Janks was sentenced to twenty-five years in prison.

CHAPTER 4
THE LEG THING

After saying goodnight to his family and retiring to his bedroom, fourteen-year-old Chris Steiner could no longer hear the July 4th fireworks as they faded into the night. He climbed into his comfortable bed as the excitement of the evening continued to play in his head. He had no idea that this night would change both his life and the lives of those around him forever.

———

The peaceful Wisconsin town of Baraboo was bathed in a warm glow as the sun rose over it. It was 1994, and July 5 marked a day of fresh starts for young Chris. He had a new job lined up and was scheduled to start that morning. At 6:15, his father, George Steiner, got up on time as the smell of breakfast filled the house. Expecting Chris to join the family at the table, he called out for him but got no response.

When George entered Chris' room, his voice fell upon empty space. Confusion gave way to concern as he realized his son was nowhere to be found. Panic gripped his heart as he frantically searched the house, hoping to locate Chris and calm the growing fear.

Chris' second-floor bedroom appeared undisturbed at first glance. George then worked his way through the house to where Chris' older brother usually slept. His brother had spent the night at a friend's house, but something in the brother's room caught George's attention—an unusual sight that sent a chill down his spine. The window screen had been deliberately cut from the outside. It was clear someone had entered the house during the night.

The realization struck George like a bolt of lightning. The front door, always locked securely each night, was unlocked. George's mind raced with myriad thoughts, seeking answers to this perplexing puzzle.

As his eyes scanned the room, they fell upon muddy footprints imprinted on the bedroom carpet. Questions flooded his mind. Who had been in their home? What had happened during the night? The answers eluded him, leaving only speculation and growing unease.

Attempting to make sense of the situation, George considered that one of Chris' friends might have entered through the window. Perhaps they had awakened Chris and lured him away for a late-night adventure, such as an illicit swim on a warm summer night. However, this explanation appeared increasingly improbable, given Chris' job the following day. It just wasn't something Chris would do.

The arrival of the police brought hope, but their initial investigations couldn't definitively determine whether Chris had run away from home. It was a possibility they couldn't rule out entirely, but deep down, George Steiner knew it was doubtful. Chris was a good-natured, responsible teenager, and there had been no recent conflicts or disagreements that could have led him to run away from home.

———

The police, family, and friends conducted relentless searches throughout the following days. The tight-knit community of Baraboo rallied together, combing every corner, every possible hiding place, and every stretch of land and water for any sign of Chris. The atmosphere was heavy with worry and concern as the days turned into nights, with no clue about his whereabouts.

Then, six agonizing days after his disappearance, the weight of despair came crashing down upon them. Chris' lifeless body was discovered draped over a partially-submerged tree stump, its branches reaching out like skeletal fingers on the edge of a Wisconsin River Sandbar. The sight was both haunting and devastating.

The authorities conducted a thorough examination, hoping to shed light on the circumstances surrounding Chris' tragic death, but the autopsy yielded few results. There were no signs of traumatic injuries on his body, and the presence of water in his lungs indicated that he had drowned. However, the cause of death was officially listed as "undetermined." It was a classification that only deepened the mystery and left the community grasping for answers.

Chris' father, George, knew his son well. He vehemently insisted that Chris was an excellent swimmer, casting doubt on the accidental drowning theory. Furthermore, none of

Chris' friends came forward to claim they had accompanied him that fateful night, further clouding the already murky situation.

Baraboo, once a serene town, now found itself grappling with shock and sorrow. The loss of a vibrant young life had struck at the core of their tightly-knit community. Rumors swirled, speculation ran rampant, and each passing day seemed to unravel more threads of confusion. Chris' grief-stricken family were left with aching hearts, burdened by a growing list of questions for which there were no immediate answers.

———

A year had passed since the haunting death of Chris Steiner when thirteen-year-old Thad Phillips fell asleep watching television in his living room. The rest of his family were asleep in their bedrooms when Thad felt himself being lifted from the floor. Assuming one of his parents was carrying him to his bedroom, he began to stir. Groggily, he opened his eyes to find himself in an unfamiliar and disorienting setting —outside his house, engulfed by darkness, and with a young man at his side.

Confusion consumed Thad as he realized he was being forcefully dragged down the sidewalk by a young man he had never seen before. The stranger insisted they run together, their footsteps echoing in the night. Thad, still dazed and half-asleep, complied without fully understanding why.

Introducing himself as Joe, the mysterious companion offered no explanation for their abrupt escape into the night. Thad's mind swirled with questions, but the urgency in Joe's voice compelled him to follow along, his young legs carrying him through the dimly-lit streets.

Their journey led them to a decrepit house which was a shadow of its former self, standing as a testament to neglect and despair. As Thad stepped inside, Joe forcefully pushed him through the door and dragged him up the stairs, into a back bedroom.

Thrown onto a lone, soiled mattress in the corner of the room, Thad's confusion morphed into fear. His heart raced as he realized the gravity of what was happening. Panic surged through his veins, but before he could react, Joe pounced on the young boy. With vicious intensity, he began to twist and turn Thad's ankle, each agonizing movement bringing searing pain.

Thad's world shattered as he felt the sickening snap of his ankle breaking from the extreme force inflicted by the older boy. The room seemed to spin as his cries for help went unheard.

In the face of unspeakable torment, Thad Phillips summoned the will to fight back. With sheer determination, he managed to break free and limped down the stairs as fast as he could. But with his ankle broken, Joe quickly caught up to him. He grabbed Thad and threw him onto a nearby couch, his anger evident in his actions.

Driven by a sickening desire to inflict pain, Joe pushed Thad's leg toward his head, applying his full body weight until the young boy's thigh snapped under the unbearable pressure. Throughout the long and harrowing night, Thad endured Joe's relentless torture, his body and spirit pushed to their limits.

Joe's demeanor would shift in twisted moments, vacillating between tormentor and occasional caregiver. He took the time to dress Thad's wounds with makeshift splints fashioned from socks and ace bandages, as if a cruel facade of compassion blended with an extreme need for violence. When Thad asked him why he was doing this to him, Joe replied coldly,

> "I'm just fascinated with the sound of breaking bones."

As the night wore on, Joe's perception of Thad as a potential threat diminished. He left the young boy alone in the upstairs room and left the house. Bruised, broken, and engulfed in unimaginable pain, Thad summoned every ounce of strength to drag his battered body out of the room and down the stairs. He knew his life depended on getting out of that house, no matter what it took.

Thad managed to drag himself down the stairs and into the kitchen, but he froze when he heard Joe return to the house with a girl. Joe and the girl settled on the couch—the girl blissfully unaware of the nightmarish ordeal unfolding in other parts of the house. Time passed, and when the girl departed, Joe's sinister attention returned to finding Thad again.

A rush of adrenaline coursed through Thad's veins as he lay silently on the kitchen floor, his breath shallow and his pain all-consuming. But inevitably, Joe discovered him and dragged him back upstairs to continue the relentless cycle of torture. Thad's legs became the target of Joe's sadistic rage, each blow inflicting new depths of agony upon the young boy. Joe warned the boy that if he tried to escape again, he'd kill him, but Thad knew that was probably his intention all along. Thad knew that if he wanted to live, he needed to somehow get out of that house.

————

Thad found himself trapped once again when Joe locked him in the bedroom closet on the evening of July 30. However, Thad's unyielding determination refused to be extinguished. He thought to himself, "I'm not going to die here." In the suffocating darkness, his searching hands stumbled upon an old, heavy guitar.

Once he knew that Joe was gone, Thad summoned every ounce of his inner strength. Swinging the guitar with relentless force, he struck the closet door repeatedly, each blow resonating with his overwhelming willpower. The door groaned in protest until it finally shattered into fragments, freeing him from his claustrophobic prison.

Thad threw himself down the stairs in agony, relying solely on his arms as his legs dragged erratically behind him. In spite of the excruciating pain that threatened to destroy him, he kept going. Thad lost consciousness several times as he went down the stairs and made his way into the kitchen.

Finally, after what felt like an eternity, Thad reached the kitchen. There, a glimmer of hope materialized in the form of a phone attached to the wall, its long cord dangling temptingly. Thad gripped the cord, and with a strong pull, the receiver broke free and clattered to the ground.

Time stood still as Thad's trembling fingers dialed 911, his voice quivering but determined as he told the operator where he was and what had happened to him.

Officers quickly responded to the distress call, storming into the house to rescue Thad from his forty-three-hour captivity. They found him in a state of unimaginable suffering, his legs shattered and broken.

As Thad began his long and arduous road to recovery, he mustered the strength to share his harrowing ordeal with the police. The name "Joe" lingered on his lips, the only identity he knew of his tormentor. Thad told detectives that Joe had not only subjected him to unspeakable horrors but had also mentioned brutalizing two other boys, one of whom was named Chris. Investigators knew he was speaking of Chris Steiner.

———

Seventeen-year-old Joe Clark was swiftly arrested following Thad's rescue. A search of Clark's home yielded a disturbing discovery—a list of boy's names. This chilling document was divided into three sections: "Get to Now," "Can Wait," and "Leg Thing."

Clark faced his first trial for the assault on Thad Phillips, and during the proceedings, he pleaded no contest to charges of attempted first-degree intentional homicide, causing great bodily harm to a child, mayhem, causing mental harm to a child, and one count of child enticement. The court handed down a severe sentence of 100 years in prison for his brutal assault. Although he pleaded no contest, Clark claimed to have no recollection of the incident.

The Steiner case took a different turn, as Clark pleaded not guilty when confronted with the charges. However, the exhumation of Chris Steiner's body provided crucial evidence. It revealed that Steiner had suffered ankle injuries strikingly similar to those inflicted on Thad Phillips. This revelation presented a damning link between the two cases, raising suspicions that Clark was involved in both abductions.

Clark's parents testified in his defense, asserting that their son had been at home, sound asleep in his room, on the night of Chris Steiner's death. However, their testimony failed to hold up against the weight of other witnesses' accounts. These witnesses attested that Clark frequently snuck out of the house through an upstairs window, creating doubt around his alibi.

The trial in the murder of Chris Steiner took a decisive turn when a former fellow inmate from Clark's time in juvenile detention provided damning testimony. She claimed that Clark had confessed to her, admitting that he had killed a boy and left his body draped over a tree. This new information hit home with the jury, making them even more sure that Clark killed Chris Steiner.

The weight of the evidence presented in court left little room for doubt. Witnesses, forensic findings, and Clark's incriminating statements vividly depicted his involvement in the heinous crime. On November 7, 1997, Clark was found guilty of first-degree homicide, mayhem, and causing great bodily harm to a child. He was sentenced to life in prison plus an additional forty years, with no chance of parole for sixty years.

———

Thad Phillips was awarded $21 million by the court, but after almost thirty years and countless surgeries, he's never seen a dime. A Go-Fund-Me campaign was set up in his name in 2023.

https://www.gofundme.com/f/support-thad-phillips-real-hero-of-baraboo

CHAPTER 5
THE SANTA FE STRANGLER

The moon hung low in the darkened New Mexico sky on November 11, 1983. It was long past checkout time when a maid made her way to room 205 at the Comfort Inn, a sleepy motel on the outskirts of Santa Fe. Her hands were filled with cleaning supplies as she knocked on the door, but there was no response. The girl staying in the room had not notified the front desk that she had checked out yet, and the maid had an uneasy feeling as she unlocked the door and stepped over the threshold. She was met with a sight that would haunt her nightmares for the rest of her life. A young woman, just twenty-two years old, lay face-down on the bed with her head hanging over the edge. Her lifeless form was contorted into a macabre display. Blood stained the once-pristine sheets, casting an ominous ugliness across the room.

Fear gripped the housekeeper, and she wasted no time reaching for the nearest phone. The emergency operator listened intently as the frightened woman's voice relayed the grisly scene she had stumbled upon. Santa Fe police were quickly dispatched, their sirens wailing through the night as they raced toward the motel.

Hearts heavy with dread, the first officers on the scene approached the lifeless figure sprawled on the bed. A red handkerchief was wound tightly around her neck, showing that she had been strangled.

Her hands, bound tightly behind her back with a pillowcase, spoke volumes about the sadistic nature of her assailant. Though her clothes remained intact, her belt buckle had been undone, leading investigators to believe there was a sexual motivation for the crime.

The young woman's red and white Nike shoes and her discarded bra lay carelessly between the two queen-sized beds.

But the thirty puncture wounds beneath the handkerchief would give investigators nightmares for the rest of their lives. It showed the sadistic nature of the crime. While some wounds were shallow and intended to inflict pain, others were deeper; they had punctured veins and arteries.

As the detectives in Santa Fe delved deeper into the brutal attack, they encountered confusing details that left them with more questions than answers. The victim received thirty stab wounds, demonstrating extreme rage. Had the killer known the girl? But more puzzling was the surprisingly small amount of blood in the room, which initially led investigators to believe the murder took place elsewhere.

Oddly, aside from the bed where the body was left, there were no indications of a struggle. It seemed the perpetrator had gone to great lengths to leave no other signs of their presence in the room. The victim's unopened suitcases suggested she had just arrived at the Comfort Inn before her tragic death.

Inside the victim's purse, the detectives found her driver's license, which showed that she was Janet Benoit, a 22-year-old from Arvada, Colorado, just outside Denver. Janet was only supposed to spend one night in Santa Fe before heading to her new job at a sporting goods store in Phoenix, Arizona, about 500 miles away.

Among her personal belongings, detectives found a rental agreement from U-Haul, indicating that she had rented a trailer for her journey. Her car, parked downstairs with the U-Haul trailer hitched to its bumper, presented no immediate signs of suspicion. The vehicle and trailer appeared untouched.

As the investigation broadened, detectives considered three potential theories regarding the killer's identity. The first theory suggested that the killer may have been an employee of the Comfort Inn—someone who exploited their position to access the victim's room. The second theory revolved around the possibility that Janet had been acquainted with her assailant, a person from her past who harbored a dark and violent resentment. The third theory proposed that the attacker had simply followed Janet, seizing the opportunity to force their way into the room as soon as she opened the door.

––––––

With the medical examiner's disturbing findings as a guide, the investigation into Janet Benoit's brutal murder continued. The coroner's report revealed that Janet had been sexually assaulted despite being fully clothed. For some reason, the killer allowed her to put her clothes back on after the attack. There was no denying the biological evidence that proved she had been raped.

The medical examiner's report also shed light on the mysterious lack of blood in the motel room. Most of the stab wounds occurred postmortem, showing the killer's rage and sadistic nature. The coroner believed that the assailant had raped her, allowed her to get dressed, fatally strangled her with the handkerchief, and then stabbed her thirty times. It was a chilling sequence of events that pointed to a deeply disturbed individual with pent-up anger and a twisted desire for power.

Armed with this new understanding, the detectives intensified their efforts, piecing together Janet's final hours. They interviewed her grieving family and the employees of the Comfort Inn, striving to establish a timeline.

————

Her family told police that Janet had planned to drive from Arvada to Phoenix, a distance of 900 miles, in one day. However, because she got a late start that morning, it was clear that she wouldn't reach her destination before dark. So, she decided to stop in Santa Fe halfway to her destination to find a safe place to stay as the sun went down.

Her final known stop before the event that would end her life was at a nearby Denny's restaurant, where she had a hamburger and fries for dinner. A waitress from the restaurant remembered seeing Janet that night at around 8:00.

The detectives discovered that Janet's car had a full tank of gas, which meant she had recently stopped at a gas station.

The motel desk clerk claimed that, at 9:30 p.m., Janet checked in alone, left the office, and walked the dimly-lit walkways to her upstairs room. After that, no further sightings or interactions were reported, and no one at the motel that night heard any commotion or cries for help. The detectives' haunting realization that the perpetrator might have entered the room using a key raised the unsettling possibility of an employee's complicity.

The detectives focused their attention on the Comfort Inn staff as they dug deeper into the brutal murder of Janet Benoit. One of them, a bartender, emerged with a disturbing tale that had everyone on edge.

The bartender revealed an alarming encounter she had experienced with the hotel manager just a month prior. In a state of intoxication, the manager tried to force himself on her, cornering her in a supply closet. She managed to fend him off only through her courage and resistance. This information painted a disturbing picture, suggesting that the manager was capable of acts of sexual violence.

The detectives wasted no time checking the manager's background. Glen Gillman, 53 years old, possessed a reputation for aggression toward women and a troubling history of run-ins with the law. He had a previous felony conviction for stabbing someone with a knife and had recently been released from prison.

Bringing Glen Gillman in for questioning, the detectives confronted him with the allegations. However, Gillman vehemently denied any involvement in Janet's murder, presenting a seemingly solid alibi. He claimed to have been attending a Bible study class at the time of the crime. The detectives arranged for him to undergo a polygraph examination while investigators verified his alibi. To their dismay,

Gillman passed the polygraph test. Later, his alibi was corroborated, and the detectives found themselves back at square one.

———

Over a year passed, and Janet's case remained unsolved when another chilling murder occurred in a motel room four hours away in Carlsbad, New Mexico. The victim, a twenty-two-year-old woman, met a fate eerily similar to Janet's. Detectives now faced the disturbing realization that a potential serial killer was on the loose.

However, their focus quickly shifted when they apprehended a suspect in the Carlsbad murder. Wayne Allen Clarke, in custody and in possession of a knife, had confessed to the crime. Detectives couldn't help but consider the possibility that Clarke may have been responsible for Janet Benoit's murder as well, since the two crimes seemed so closely related.

Detectives looked into Wayne Allen Clarke's background, hoping to uncover any potential links to Janet's murder. Their search led them to discover that Clarke had once worked at a Denny's restaurant, the very same chain where Janet had eaten her final meal.

However, as the police questioned Clarke, it became apparent that he had worked at a different Denny's location —not the one in Santa Fe. Furthermore, his work records and alibi confirmed that, on the night of Janet's murder, he was employed at a hotel 300 miles away. With no tangible evidence linking Clarke to Janet's murder, the investigators had to redirect their focus once again.

———

Just seven months after Janet's murder, the murder of Teri Mulvaney, a 25-year-old secretary, sent shockwaves through the community of Santa Fe. The striking similarities between Teri's brutal slaying and the earlier murder of Janet Benoit raised unsettling questions and fueled suspicions that a dangerous predator was preying on innocent young women.

Teri's family held steadfast in their belief that their neighbor, David Bruce Morton, was responsible for her death. They recounted how Morton had visited Teri's Galisteo Street home, wanting to use her telephone the night before she was murdered. Teri was familiar with Morton, and she had heard rumors that he was an ex-convict. She had confided in her friends that she felt uneasy around him and even feared him. It was disheartening to learn that Morton had been released from prison only a year before Teri's murder, following a conviction for armed robbery.

Morton was already in jail on a drunk driving charge when he was charged with Teri's murder. His cellmate came forward, sharing that Morton had confessed to killing Teri. However, despite the cellmate's disturbing revelation, the prosecutors deemed the evidence insufficient to bring charges against Morton for the murder.

Teri's family didn't let this setback stop them from fighting for justice. Because they were sure Morton was guilty, they worked hard to get more than 2,000 signatures supporting a grand jury investigation. The trial ended, however, with Morton being found not guilty by eleven of the twelve jurors.

Following his acquittal, David Bruce Morton departed Santa Fe, making his way to Amarillo, Texas. Tragically, on May 4,

1990, he committed another horrific crime. Kim Kendall, a 22-year-old secretary and college student who lived near Morton, fell victim to his violent urges. She was raped, strangled, and stabbed. Her devastated husband discovered her lifeless body. Like Janet Benoit and Teri Mulvaney, Kendall had been stabbed post-mortem.

A mere two months before Kendall's murder, her apartment had been burglarized, and the police discovered a fingerprint that matched that of David Bruce Morton. Swiftly apprehended, Morton faced justice, but not for murder—instead, he was convicted of burglary. However, he received a life sentence due to his habitual offender status. Three years later, in 1993, he faced yet another trial and was found guilty of Kim Kendall's murder, ultimately receiving a sentence of 174 years behind bars.

———

Back in Santa Fe, the murders of Janet Benoit and Teri Mulvaney remained unsolved. In 1995, David Benoit, Janet's brother, sought the assistance of private investigator George Seibel, a former Chicago homicide detective, in his relentless pursuit of justice for his sister. Seibel delved into the details of Janet's murder and made a crucial observation. Most often, when a knife is used to attack the neck, the intent is to slash. However, Janet's injuries consisted solely of puncture wounds—a highly unusual characteristic. Seibel recognized the significance of this distinction, realizing that they needed to focus their search on cases where the neck had been punctured rather than sliced, as it could potentially lead them to their sister's killer. Little did they know that uncovering the truth would be a lengthy and arduous journey spanning several decades.

After eight years of relentless investigation, Seibel finally drew a connection between the murder of Kim Kendall and the striking similarities it shared with Janet Benoit's case. David Benoit, who was now persuaded of the significance of the information, made contact with the Santa Fe police department once more and pleaded with them to reopen the investigation into the death of his sister. He suggested they concentrate on David Bruce Morton and reconsider the possibility that he was involved in Janet's murder.

————

During the investigation into David Morton's movements on the evening of Janet's murder, the Santa Fe police department discovered a fascinating insight from David Morton's wife. She told detectives she wasn't with him when Janet was killed because she was out of town. Despite this, she vividly recalled a discussion with David the following day as they drove past the Comfort Inn.

They were driving by the motel when their attention was drawn to the unmistakable yellow crime scene tape. She curiously turned to David and asked what he thought had happened, but his response made her uneasy. David, whose nerves were clearly frazzled and seemed to be in a state of disorder, yelled at her nervously, "It's nothing! Just keep going! Just drive!"

Further adding to their case, a cellmate of David Bruce Morton in Amarillo contacted the detectives, alleging that David had shared details of his involvement in the killings of two women in Santa Fe.

Nevertheless, the detectives faced an uphill battle, lacking concrete physical evidence linking Morton to the Santa Fe murders. Sadly, after almost twenty years, any biological traces that could have aided their investigation had long since degraded. Left with limited alternatives, their focus shifted to Amarillo, where they sought to interview David Morton.

––––––

On February 7, 2003, within the confines of the Amarillo penitentiary, Santa Fe detectives embarked on a pivotal interview with David Bruce Morton. Initially, Morton vehemently denied any involvement in the gruesome murders. However, after hours of arduous interrogation that tested the limits of their investigative skills, Morton finally succumbed to the pressure. He confessed to the Santa Fe detectives that he was indeed responsible for the murders of Janet Benoit and Teri Mulvaney.

Morton described how he had been driving through the streets of Santa Fe when Janet Benoit, who was filling up her gas tank, caught his attention. Intrigued, he shadowed her movements until she arrived at the motel. Watching her check in and unload her belongings, he trailed behind her as she walked up the staircase to the second floor. Seizing the moment, he forcibly entered the motel room after her, his hand firmly clamping over her mouth to muffle her terrified screams.

According to his chilling account, Morton used a steak knife to subdue his victim. He then forced her onto the bed and sexually assaulted her. Once he finished, Janet pleaded with him to allow her to dress. Recognizing her impending fate, she implored him not to leave her lifeless body unclothed for the world to discover. Morton allowed her to get dressed, bound her with torn pillowcases, and secured her wrists tightly behind her back.

He disclosed how he ruthlessly stabbed Janet thirty times after first strangling her with a handkerchief he had brought along.

After nineteen years of longing for a resolution, the families of Janet Benoit and Teri Mulvaney finally obtained a semblance of closure.

Feeling the weight of his unpardonable acts, David Bruce Morton entered a guilty plea and apologized to the court on February 11, 2004.

Several other murders of young women in the Santa Fe area remain unsolved, and David Bruce Morton is still the prime suspect in each of them.

- Teal Pittington, who was only 18 years old, went missing in August 1984. In March 1985, her decomposed body was found in a ditch near Lamy. Dental records were required to verify her identity.
- Susan LaPorte, a 25-year-old from Boston, visited Santa Fe in December 1985 to see a friend. Tragically, her life was cut short. A patrol officer found her lifeless body under a juniper tree. A rope was tightly knotted around her neck and wrists. A retired FBI agent, who now works for the Bernalillo County Sheriff's Department cold case squad, found a DNA link between LaPorte's case and the semen sample from the Padilla case in 2009. Still, no one was ever arrested in connection with these crimes.
- In August 1987, Michelle Quintana, a 23-year-old real estate worker, disappeared without a trace. Her truck

was found at the DeVargas Center mall, and witnesses said they saw her get into a red Jeep with two men. Even though her body was never found, the circumstances strongly suggested that she, too, had met a tragic end.

These disturbing incidents further fueled the rumors that a serial killer was terrorizing New Mexico. No one has been arrested in connection with these murders.

CHAPTER 6
VANISHED INNOCENCE

In 1962, just two days after Christmas, the quiet Rockwood neighborhood in east Portland, Oregon, was about to be shaken by a distressing event that would haunt its residents for years. The morning of December 27 began like every other Saturday for the family of Mona Rae Minyard. Six-year-old Mona Rae and her two brothers were glued to the television, watching their favorite Saturday morning cartoons.

Mona's mother, Joyce Lane, needed a few groceries, and Mona jumped at the chance to help. The young girl's eyes lit up as she begged her mother to let her go. She and her brothers had been to the Three Brothers Market many times. It was only a few blocks away, across a small field, but Joyce didn't want to make the trip herself because she was pregnant. Even though she wouldn't usually let her daughter go alone, Mona was so eager to help that she reluctantly agreed to let her do the simple job on her own.

Shortly before noon, Joyce placed a $5 bill in a light blue envelope along with a list containing the essentials for their dinner: ground beef, bread, cheese, and milk. Mona Rae Minyard took the envelope and walked across the street toward the Three Brothers Market wearing a checkered skirt, a gray coat, black shoes, white socks, and a blue scarf highlighting her blonde hair and blue eyes.

No one realized it would be the last time Mona would see her family or the Rockwood neighborhood. The streets swallowed her up, and her absence grew into an unsettling void as the hours went by. The disappearance of the innocent six-year-old girl cast a dark shadow over the Rockwood neighborhood.

The police acted immediately and began a massive search of the area. The effort included the participation of law enforcement, concerned residents, and volunteers who combed the area in search of any indication that the little girl had once been there. But hours stretched into days, and despite the hopes of those concerned and the ceaseless efforts of those involved, Mona's disappearance remained a mystery.

As the initial shock and disbelief began to subside, the people of Portland were left grappling with questions that seemed to have no answers. What had happened to Mona Rae Minyard such a short distance from her home, in broad daylight? Had someone deliberately snatched her from the neighborhood streets? The only certainty was the heartbreaking truth that Mona, the young girl with a radiant smile and promising future, had vanished without a trace.

———

The Portland community was in a state of fear and uncertainty following the disappearance of Mona Rae

Minyard. The local authorities, driven by an unwavering determination to unravel the truth, left no stone unturned in their quest for answers. Their first action was to reach out to Mona's friends, hoping to find any leads that might shed light on her whereabouts.

Initially, investigators entertained the possibility that Mona had made her intended purchases at the Three Brothers Market. An employee from the market claimed to have seen a young girl matching Mona's description buying similar items. However, as the investigation progressed, it became evident that their hopes had been misplaced. Another girl had actually made purchases similar to those on the shopping list, but it wasn't Mona. She never made it to the market. Somewhere along her intended route, Mona vanished without a trace.

As more confusing accounts surfaced, the reality became more and more muddled. One witness came forward and described seeing a young girl and a dog at the store. However, Mona's parents insisted their dog hadn't left the house that day. The conflicting testimonies deepened the confusion surrounding Mona's disappearance.

Joyce Lane couldn't face the chilling truth, because the weight of her daughter's absence was too much for her to bear. She was so sad and hopeless that she had to be sedated to protect her fragile spirit from the full impact of the tragedy.

As the year came to an end, New Year's Eve would always be remembered as a dark moment in Portland's history. That afternoon, two men looking at a property they planned to buy as an investment made a horrifying discovery. The lifeless body of Mona Rae Minyard was found in a drainage ditch. Partially dressed and robbed of her innocence, she was a victim of unspeakable violence.

Law enforcement wasted no time in cordoning off the grim scene. Mona's tiny body was carefully transported to the morgue, where forensic examiners embarked on the solemn task of conducting an autopsy. Through their meticulous examination, the truth emerged. Mona had suffered the unimaginable fate of being raped, strangled, and thrown away like trash.

———

Gresham's Forest Lawn Cemetery became the backdrop for the final chapter of Mona Rae Minyard's young life. Mona lay peacefully in her casket, dressed in her favorite outfit—a red poodle skirt, a white blouse, and white boots. Clutched in her hands was her cherished Kissy Doll, symbolizing the joy she had experienced on Christmas morning, just days before tragedy struck.

Attending the service, Joyce Lane, visibly pregnant, donned a maternity dress as she joined the sea of mourners. The weight of sorrow hung in the air, filling the space with an unspoken heaviness.

———

During the investigation into the brutal rape and murder of Mona Rae Minyard, the spotlight of suspicion shone squarely on one man: Joseph Walton Holmes. Holmes was one of the first people who came to mind as a suspect because his house was near Mona's, just across a grassy field.

Eleven hours before Mona's body was discovered, at 3:30 a.m., Holmes was detained by police while wandering the streets near her residence. Holmes claimed he was drunk and bar-hopping, but his presence in the area made police suspicious. When he was taken in for questioning, he was given a thorough strip search to look for clues such as scratches or bloodstains, but the search turned up nothing. Holmes denied that he had ever met Mona, and he said he didn't even know her name.

Attempting to determine his potential involvement, investigators gave Holmes a lie detector test on New Year's Day. To their surprise, the results indicated he was telling the truth, further clouding their suspicions. However, a tip from a neighbor prompted detectives to delve deeper into Holmes' life, leading them to search his car in February. The diligent forensic team collected and analyzed fibers from the vehicle, ultimately uncovering a chilling revelation. The fibers matched material found on Mona's body, and a hair found in his car appeared to match hers.

The search for answers led detectives to Holmes' wife, who revealed a startling piece of information. She claimed her husband was well acquainted with Mona and had spoken to her several times. A troubling picture started to take shape, pointing to a more intimate relationship between Holmes and the young victim than was previously thought. Additional research into Holmes' past revealed a concerning mental health component. Doctors who treated him at the Portland Veterans Hospital confirmed that he had the mental capacity of an adolescent and regularly suffered from memory lapses connected to situations he considered embarrassing.

Detectives used sodium pentothal, a barbiturate known to lower inhibitions, as a "truth serum" during a later round of interrogations. Holmes, however, unexpectedly refused to answer any more questions after being shown the evidence that connected him to the murder and claimed he was being held against his will. Since there were no solid grounds for keeping him in custody and no clear answers to their suspicions, investigators had no choice but to release him.

But when a worried mother contacted the police and revealed a shocking discovery about Holmes' conduct, the course of the inquiry unexpectedly changed. The woman said that Holmes tended to act inappropriately toward young girls in the neighborhood, especially Mona. He allegedly held the children on his lap while playing with dolls and involved them in uncomfortable activities like "playing doctor."

A ray of hope appeared for Joyce Lane in late March when investigators informed her of their intention to arrest Holmes on suspicion of child abuse. Yet her hopes were short-lived. Six days later, Holmes was released when a witness failed to correctly identify him in a lineup. It was a catastrophic setback for the efforts to bring Mona's killer to justice.

———

The pain in Sam Lane's heart had not lessened with time. Still suffering from the loss of his cherished stepdaughter, Mona, he sought refuge in the shadows of a Portland pub. He found himself nursing a drink and lost in a dark reflection of the past. In a cruel twist of fate, Joseph Walton Holmes walked into the bar, worsening his agony. Sam quickly recognized him, his pulse racing with a combination of rage and sorrow. Sam immediately left the pub, unable to handle seeing the man accused of destroying his family.

Yet a few days later, Sam returned to the same bar with desperation in his eyes. He waited in his vehicle outside the bar's entrance, this time with a loaded shotgun on the passenger seat. His goal was clear: he would not let Holmes get away a second time. He was ready to face the man who, for too long, had gotten away with killing his little girl. However, while he sat there, his mind wandered to the children he still had. He wanted to make sure they had the future he never had. He forced down his frustration and drove home, opting for the more responsible and selfless way.

———

Time dragged on as the months turned into years, then the years into decades. The Lanes left Portland and its terrible memories behind to put their lives back together. The case, once a hotbed of eager inquiry, had since cooled. The family began to accept the idea that justice would never come their way since time seemed determined to bury the truth.

Then, a glimmer of hope emerged on a Friday night in 2008. As the Lane family returned home from their grandson's football game, their wearied hearts were met with an unexpected message on their answering machine. The voice on the other end identified itself as Maurice Delehant, a detective with the Clackamas County Sheriff's Office. His words reverberated through the room, stirring emotions that had lain dormant for forty-five long years. Joyce Lane, trembling with a mixture of anticipation and apprehension, understood that this call could unlock the truth surrounding Mona's disappearance.

———

When they called back, Detective Delehant told Sam and Joyce that, due to developments in DNA testing and the need to provide comfort to bereaved relatives, the unsolved murder investigation of Mona Rae Minyard had been reopened. Mona's case was the second-oldest of the county's thirteen unsolved murder cases.

When Delehant looked through the case files, he found a treasure trove of information: 900 old, fragile pages that told the story of the investigation. Delehant was born the same year Mona died, and he felt a personal stake in doing what was right. He, too, was the father of young girls, and the weight of the tragedy hit him hard.

When Delehant returned to the neighborhood of Rockwood, which he used to know well, he found that the area had changed. Restaurants, apartments, and the city's light rail system stood in place of Mona's family home and the field she crossed to get to the market. The community had changed physically over the years, but the memories of Mona's disappearance were still deeply ingrained in the hearts of the people who had known her.

When Delehant dug further into the specifics of the investigation, he came upon a disturbing discovery. Throughout the proceedings of Holmes' prosecution for the sexual assault of a child, his brother had accompanied him in court, dressing almost identically and sporting haircuts that were quite similar to Holmes'. When the police put Holmes in a lineup, his brother was also in it. The case was dropped because the two girls couldn't agree on who the criminal was when they were shown the suspects to choose from. Although such a situation would not be acceptable in the court system today, the defense used it at the time as a sneaky tactic. Delehant also learned that Holmes was killed in a vehicle accident in 1967, just five short years after Mona's murder.

Still in search of justice, Delehant looked through the evidence locker at the warehouse in Oregon City and found a cardboard box full of old items. Mona's blue and white gingham dress, black shoes, and gray wool coat were among those items. They were tangible reminders of a life that had been taken away so quickly. Scientists carefully examined the dress' fabric at the Oregon State Police Forensic Lab for signs of sperm stains. However, time had done its damage, and the DNA had long since broken down, leaving them with nothing. Other things in the collection were mislabeled or mixed up, which made them impossible to analyze effectively. Samples of dirt and hair were taken, but without the proper paperwork, it was impossible to figure out what they meant. The evidence was reluctantly put back in the locker, where its secrets would remain hidden.

———

In 2009, Detective Delehant's dogged determination led him to devise a new plan to solve the Mona Rae Minyard case, which had been on his mind and in his life for years now. He contacted the senior investigator at the Clackamas County District Attorney's office and asked for something special. Delehant was confident that Joseph Walton Holmes was to blame for Mona's tragic death, so he asked the senior investigator to look into the case and come to the same conclusion that he and the investigators at the time had reached: that Holmes was to blame. His ultimate goal was to end the case and give the Lane family peace.

But there were obstacles. The biggest problems were that the suspect had died, and the detectives who had worked on the case before had also died. In 2010, a jury would have to rely on witnesses if there wasn't any forensic evidence to show them. However, there were no witnesses. There was no way his request could be approved.

Determined to give the Lane family some semblance of closure and to honor their tireless pursuit of justice, Delehant sought permission to provide copies of all the evidence to Joyce Lane and to return Mona's clothes to her. He believed the Lanes needed to at least understand how diligently the investigators had worked on the case and the extent of their efforts.

————

On March 17, 2010, Delehant received the long-awaited approval. He embarked on a journey to the Lane family's home in Seneca, Oregon, carrying the three black binders filled with evidence and Mona's cherished clothes.

As Delehant handed the binders to Joyce, tears welled up in her eyes. The weight of decades of sorrow and uncertainty lifted, if only for a fleeting moment. She held Mona's clothes close, feeling the tangible connection to her lost daughter. In that bittersweet exchange, Delehant shared what he had discovered about Holmes bringing his brother to the lineup, eliminating the chance of his conviction. While Holmes would never face justice in a court of law, Joyce Lane found relief in the knowledge that the man believed by many to be her daughter's murderer was now deceased.

Though the pursuit of justice had not yielded the desired outcome, the Lane family found a sense of closure—a bittersweet peace in knowing that Mona's case had been meticulously examined, and her memory would not be forgotten.

The black binders and Mona's clothes served as a reminder of the dedication and unwavering determination of those who had relentlessly sought the truth.

CHAPTER 7
BLOODSTAINED SECRETS

May 2017 marked the discovery of a lifeless body in the basement of a suburban home, a victim of a brutal gunshot wound to the head. Police in the small town of Bel-Air, Ohio, were summoned to the scene, only to find themselves entangled in a web of intrigue and deceit.

When the police arrived, David Kinney, his wife Cheri, and their daughter were there waiting for them. The family had been longtime friends of the deceased, Brad McGarry.

Cheri and David Kinney were overcome with emotion, tears streaming down their faces as they described the shocking scene they had stumbled upon. They had known Brad for nine years and considered him an integral part of their family. Brad and David had become best friends after they met during coal mining classes years prior, forming an unbreakable bond. They had even planned a family trip to the Bahamas in August.

David trembled as he explained to police officers that the family had gone down to the basement to deliver a weed eater when they made the horrifying discovery. Their daughter had knocked on the front door with no response, so they tried the back door, which was open. Upon entering, they immediately noticed the kitchen in complete disarray, with items scattered all over. David sensed that something was terribly wrong and shared his concerns with Cheri. Their daughter then checked the basement and found Brad on the floor.

Yet, as investigators probed deeper, it became evident that there was more to this macabre tale than met the eye.

Upon peering into the basement, the officers were confronted with a chilling sight: Brad McGarry's lifeless body, sprawled on the floor, surrounded by a pool of blood encircling his head.

As they delved into Brad's death, a compelling detail emerged. Brad McGarry, an openly gay man in a conservative neighborhood, had recently ended a relationship with a man named Scotty, whose last name remained unknown. The unfolding secrets hinted at a tumultuous connection that had now culminated in a devastating tragedy.

The crime scene presented puzzling evidence. Despite the apparent disarray within the house, nothing had been taken —the absence of missing belongings cast doubt on whether it was a genuine burglary. Cell phones, big-screen TVs, and even money strewn on the floor remained untouched. The scene seemed staged.

The possibility of suicide loomed large in the investigators' minds, given the presence of a gunshot wound. However, there was a problem with that theory: there was no gun. In many instances, however, when a person commits suicide, and the gun is not visible, the most reasonable explanation is that the victim fell on it, hiding it from view. Yet, there was still no gun when Brad's body was moved. It suddenly seemed that suicide wasn't an option.

Detectives swiftly initiated interviews with Brad's circle of friends and family, piecing together timeline fragments that might lead them closer to the killer.

Scotty Butler, Brad's former boyfriend, emerged as a prime suspect. The detectives wasted no time tracking him down, only to encounter an unexpected twist: Scotty had been in jail for months. There was no way he had anything to do with Brad's murder. The pieces of this puzzle got more complicated as time went on.

Investigators then focused on the neighborhood, scouring for any surveillance footage that might shed light on the events surrounding Brad's tragic end. Their diligence paid off when a vigilant neighbor's camera captured the comings and goings near Brad's home. As they combed through hours of footage, they continued their interviews with friends and family, hoping for more clues.

During the interviews, Brad's cousin provided crucial information that would alter the course of the investigation. She recounted an incident on early Sunday, just hours before the murder, when she, Brad, and another cousin visited their grandmother's house. Brad casually mentioned that a married friend, "DJ," was coming to his home that afternoon.

It became clear that Brad felt deep, romantic feelings for DJ and had been engaging in a secret gay relationship with him for years, unbeknownst to DJ's wife.

However, the cousin's revelation held an astonishing twist. The so-called DJ was none other than David Kinney. David— a tall, masculine, and imposing figure adorned with a full beard and heavily-tattooed forearms— was having a secret, homosexual love affair with Brad. For years, Kinney had hidden his lifestyle from his wife and the conservative, small town around him. The unexpected revelation shed new light on the case.

David Kinney unknowingly became entangled in the web of suspicion. Earlier, he had mentioned to detectives that he had photos and screenshots on his phone that may be helpful to the investigation. While Kinney believed the authorities had confiscated his phone to obtain the images, they were, in fact, tracing his phone's movements on the night of the murder.

Examination of Kinney's phone's location data revealed further proof that David and Brad's relationship extended far beyond simple friendship. Despite deleting previous conversations with Brad, investigators uncovered text messages indicating they had long been hiding a covert affair.

As investigators followed the digital trail, a bone-chilling truth emerged: David's phone was at Brad's house at the time of the murder.

Reviewing the neighbor's CCTV footage, the puzzle pieces began to align. David Kinney initially arrived in his wife's car at Brad's residence, only to depart shortly after that.

Hours later, he reappeared with his family, delivering a seemingly innocuous weed eater that Brad had allegedly desired to borrow. The pieces fell into place, painting a damning portrait of David's involvement in the fateful events.

As the evidence piled up, David's innocence started to crumble. The detective employed strategic questioning techniques to build trust and unravel the web of deception. Even though David kept lying, his defenses got weaker. Overwhelmed by the weight of the evidence against him, David finally appeared to be crumbling.

With a flushed face and tears streaming down his cheeks, David Kinney recounted to detectives the tale of Brad arriving at the house accompanied by an unknown man. Then, in a sudden and jarring moment, a gunshot echoed through the air. The mysterious man had shot Brad, then hastily fled the scene in Brad's BMW.

The astute detective, however, quickly saw through David's fabrication. The front seat of Brad's car was filled with items he had recently brought home from a wedding, proving that David was lying. There was simply no space for an additional passenger in the BMW.

As David narrated the story, he consistently concealed his face—a telling sign of deception. The detective then pointed out that Brad's BMW was still parked at his house. The mysterious man that David described couldn't have taken off in the car.

———

Still, David refused to back down from his story. He insisted a mystery man had killed Brad but allowed him, the only witness to the crime, to live.

When the detective asked why he hadn't just called the police, why he had made up the elaborate story, and why he had sent his daughter into the basement to discover the body, David had no answer. Only tears.

Aware of David's propensity for deception, the detective resorted to a different interrogation approach. He crafted a fabricated scenario and suggested to David that the incident might have occurred accidentally. Planting the seed of doubt, the detective probed,

> "Maybe somebody was fucking around and accidentally shot him. And then panicked and didn't think anybody would believe him. Was it an accident? Am I right? Drop all this shit and just let it out. Brad deserves it. Brad's family deserves it. Your kids deserve it."

David's defenses crumbled in a sudden turn of events, and he confessed,

> "Brad has been pressuring me to leave my wife and kids for a while. I love my wife and kids more than anything."

David revealed that he had repeatedly informed Brad of his unwavering commitment to his family, refusing to abandon them for a relationship with Brad. David said their arguments often turned violent, with Brad resorting to physical aggression.

David acknowledged that a heated argument had taken place on that fateful Sunday. He claimed that Brad had become increasingly aggressive, raising his voice and invading David's personal space. David claimed that Brad had then pulled out a small handgun.

The detective listened attentively, coaxing David to disclose the whole truth and provide a full confession.

According to David, Brad had waved the gun threateningly, screaming that David had toyed with his emotions for too long. In a moment of desperation, David claimed that he had wrestled the gun from Brad's grasp and, in the ensuing struggle, fired the fatal shot.

But as quickly as the confession arose, David's lips sealed shut. Seeking legal counsel, he retreated, leaving many unanswered questions.

Although he admitted that he shot and killed Brad, David pleaded not guilty. The courtroom would become the stage for justice, where the puzzle of Brad McGarry's tragic end would be laid bare for all to witness.

In February 2018, the courtroom drama reached its climax. David Kinney, convicted of aggravated murder with a gun specification, stood before the judge, his fate sealed.

In court, Kinney expressed remorse for his actions that day, claiming he wished he could take it all back, yet he refrained from either confessing or providing an explanation. His words echoed with hollow remorse, a futile attempt to undo the irreversible.

At sentencing, Judge Frank Fregiato said,

> "If this man was able to do an assassin's job on someone he loved and his best friend, what could he do to his enemy or someone who opposed him?"

Regrettably, apologies alone could not resurrect the life he cruelly snuffed out. David Kinney would serve a life sentence in prison without the possibility of parole. He would ultimately languish within the cold confines of Belmont Correctional Institution, paying the price for his transgressions. At the same time, the scars of Brad McGarry's untimely demise continued to haunt those left behind.

CHAPTER 8
THE MAGNIFICENT GENTLEMAN

In the late 1980s, Peter Rodger worked as a filmmaker making television ads in London. There, he met Li Chin Tye, a nurse from Malaysia who was also working in the London film industry on the set of Indiana Jones and the Last Crusade. They were both young and passionate about their work, and they felt a strong attraction to one another. The couple fell in love quickly and were married in the early 1990s.

In 1991, Chin gave birth to their first child, Elliot, and soon after, their daughter Georgia arrived. The small family enjoyed a happy life in London, but Peter knew that if he wanted to advance his filmmaking career, he needed to be closer to Hollywood. So, in 1996, the family of four packed up and moved to sunny Los Angeles, California.

When Elliot started attending Topanga Elementary School at age five, he seemed cheerful and intelligent. However, challenges loomed ahead. When he turned seven, his parents made the painful choice to get a divorce and separate the family. This news hit Elliot hard, and he struggled to cope with the changes that followed. He and his sister had to divide their time between their mother's and father's houses, spending weekdays with their mom and weekends with their dad.

This new arrangement left Elliot feeling uncertain, withdrawn, and shy. In the early years of primary school, he attempted to fit in with the popular kids but found it difficult to make friends. The upheaval in his personal life significantly impacted his social interactions and overall confidence.

Within a year of his parents' divorce, before Elliot could fully adapt to their changed living situation, his father remarried a talented actress named Soumaya Akaaourne. Originally from Morocco, she later had a role in the Matt Damon movie, Green Zone. This new living situation intensified Elliot's anger and resentment. He frequently argued with Soumaya and adamantly refused to respect her authority. Their strained relationship persisted for several years.

Despite the shattered marriage and Elliot's unresolved anger, his parents ensured that he enjoyed a life of privilege and affluence. He often embarked on lavish family holidays abroad, visited relatives in the United Kingdom, and was provided with the finest amenities money could buy. They traveled first class, rode in luxurious limousines, stayed at upscale hotels, and dined at exclusive restaurants.

Despite having a small group of friends, Elliot's attempts to fit in with the popular crowd at school proved unsuccessful. As he entered his teenage years, he became the target of relentless bullying which only added to his challenges.

When Elliot reached the age of thirteen, his father and stepmother welcomed a new addition to the family: a half-brother. This new addition to the family only worsened Elliot's frustration and feelings of alienation. Throughout his teenage years, he turned to YouTube as an outlet for his emotions, creating a channel called "Elliot's Blog." Although the channel garnered very few views, he used it as a platform to share his childhood memories and express the over-whelming loneliness that consumed him.

The bullying at school persisted, pushing Elliot deeper into a state of depression. At one point, his tormentors even taped his head to his desk with masking tape. In his YouTube rants, he directed his resentment toward almost everyone, but particularly girls at his school who seemed indifferent to his existence.

Elliot's parents repeatedly moved him from one school to another in order to address the unrelenting harassment and cruel pranks perpetrated against him by his classmates. However, these frequent school changes hindered his ability to establish lasting connections with his peers, leaving him with only a handful of online friends.

By the time he reached the age of sixteen, Elliot had recog-nized the need for professional help and sought a psychia-trist. Doctors prescribed him potent anti-psychotic medications, but he refused to take them. Instead, he turned to his YouTube blog as a form of therapy, believing that expressing his frustrations and emotions through his videos gave him more relief than any medication ever could.

During his impassioned video rants, Elliot vented his anger and resentment toward his upbringing as the son of a Holly-wood insider. He reflected on his realization as a nine-year-old, recognizing the existence of social hierarchies and expe-riencing feelings of jealousy and envy that would haunt him throughout his life.

Interestingly, according to his father, Elliot never expressed rage as a child, only severe depression. His father was unaware of the deep-seated emotions his son had bottled up, as well as the imminent storm brewing within him.

––––––

For a brief period, Elliot became determined to turn his life around. He believed that mastering two aspects of life would be key to winning the hearts of women and salvaging his existence. He became convinced that all he needed was a nice car and a refined fashion sense. In his mind, possessing these material possessions would bridge the gap between him and the beautiful women he desired.

Elliot took a bold step, motivated by his desire to become an irresistible presence that women would be drawn to. He sold his old car and invested in a BMW, believing that driving a luxurious vehicle would enhance his appeal. In addition, he revamped his hairstyle and filled his wardrobe with expensive, designer clothing.

However, despite his newfound image, Elliot made no active attempts to forge new friendships. Instead, during lunch breaks at school, he parked his car in the parking lot and sat alone, hoping others would approach him. Unfortunately, his expectations were never met, and he remained isolated.

The disappointment and loneliness resulting from his lack of social interaction only deepened Elliot's downward spiral. Despite not making a sincere effort to connect with others at school, he grew increasingly frustrated and angry. The stark reality of his situation clashed with his unrealistic expectations.

Consumed by his resentment toward the world and its inhabitants, Elliot withdrew further into isolation, confining himself to his bedroom. As a virtual escape, he played video games like World of Warcraft and Halo, where he formed connections with three online friends named James, Philip, and Addison.

As time passed, Elliot's sadness transformed into rage. Simple displays of affection, such as couples kissing or holding hands, triggered intense bouts of hysteria within him.

At nineteen, in the summer of 2011, Elliot left his father's house and relocated to Isla Vista, a coastal town in Santa Barbara, California, where he enrolled at Santa Barbara City College. His parents hoped that the sun, sand, and college life would help him break free from his isolation. However, during this period, Elliot began meticulously planning what he called his "Day of Retribution," a horrifying scheme that he believed would be his ultimate vengeance against society.

In Isla Vista, Elliot shared an apartment with two other young men. However, it quickly became apparent to his roommates that something was wrong with Elliot. Within a month, both roommates moved out, leaving Elliot alone with his toxic thoughts.

The manifestation of Elliot's anger began to show in July 2012. He felt overwhelmed with jealousy as he watched a group of what he considered "popular college kids" laughing and having fun in a park. Elliot became irritated by their apparent happiness and impulsively drove to a nearby K-Mart store, where he bought a super soaker water gun and a bottle of orange juice.

Returning to the park, Elliot filled the toy water gun with orange juice and doused the group of kids before quickly fleeing the scene.

He later wrote,

> "I screamed at them with rage as I sprayed them with my super soaker... I was giddy with ecstatic, hate-fueled excitement."

A year later, Elliot exploded with jealousy as he watched a couple kissing as they waited in line at a Starbucks.

> "When they left the store, I followed them to their car and splashed my coffee all over them. I was panicking as I got into my car and drove off, shaking with rage-fueled excitement."

During his troubled state, Elliot became attracted to misogynistic websites which fueled his anger toward women. On the chat boards, he expressed his desire for a world where women would fear him.

Elliot's online rants delved into his sense of being different due to his mixed-race heritage. He expressed his disgust for interracial dating and made multiple racist comments, targeting African-American, South Asian, and East Asian individuals. These disturbing sentiments revealed his increasing hostility toward racial diversity and his deep-seated prejudices. He wrote,

> "Full Asian men are disgustingly ugly, and white girls would never go for you. You're just butthurt that you were born as an Asian piece of shit, so you lash out by linking these fake

pictures. You even admit that you wish you were half-white. You'll never be half-white, and you'll never fulfill your dream of marrying a white woman. I suggest you jump off a bridge."

After the departure of his previous roommates, two new young men moved into Elliot's apartment to share the rent. However, Elliot's daily interactions with them were marked by frequent arguments that sometimes turned into fights. Once again, he withdrew from social interactions and isolated himself from others.

During this period, Elliot developed an obsession with gambling. He believed winning the lottery would be the key to obtaining wealth and attracting women. In reckless pursuit of his fantasies, he spent over $100 on lottery tickets in the first week of February 2012. Disappointed by the quick lack of success, instead of accepting defeat, he became even more determined. The following week, he spent $500 on lottery tickets, then $700 the third week. He later wrote,

> "By the month of April, I had driven to Arizona three more times, making a total of four trips to Arizona in my lifetime, just to buy lottery tickets out of intense desperation, believing it to be my only hope of attaining the life I desire, the life I know I'm worthy of. I kept dreaming of the life I would have once I won; the beautiful blonde girlfriend, the luxurious mansion with a magnificent view, all of the exotic cars I would drive to impress girls. It gave me hope. It gave me something to live for."

Elliot stubbornly refused to acknowledge the fact that he was losing money, despite the fact that he did so repeatedly. He developed a sense of entitlement, believing that he was being unjustly deprived of what he thought he deserved.

As spring break approached in Isla Vista, Elliot retreated further into his bedroom, isolating himself from the outside world. Fueled by a toxic mix of anger, sadness, and over-whelming loneliness, he rarely ventured outside except to wander the streets, capturing bitter monologues on his cell phone camera and expressing his grievances about the perceived injustices in his life.

In April, one of the few individuals Elliot considered a friend, James, reached a breaking point. Unable to tolerate Elliot's pessimistic and warped views any longer, James decided to cut off contact with him. Left feeling even more isolated, Elliot turned to self-destructive behavior. Deter-mined to drown himself in self-pity, he tried to drink an entire bottle of wine but even failed at that. He accidentally spilled wine onto his laptop, rendering it unusable; this further added to his frustration and disappointment.

The day after he failed to drink himself into oblivion, Elliot found himself on a detour while driving to purchase a new laptop. He made an impulsive decision to stop at a firing range, unaware of the profound impact it would have on his life. As he held a weapon in his hand and felt the recoil, a chilling realization dawned upon him: humans were nothing more than savage animals. Believing that he was incapable of integrating into society, he concluded that his only recourse was to bring them all down.

Motivated by this twisted revelation, Elliot set out to docu-ment his dark thoughts and intentions. He began writing what would later be referred to as his manifesto. Empowered by a disturbing sense of superiority, he purchased a Glock 34 semiautomatic pistol. In his manifesto, Elliot expressed his belief that the gun made him feel like an alpha male, evoking a sense of power and control.

> "I brought it back to my room and felt a new sense of power. I was now armed. Who's the alpha male now, bitches? . . . The final solution to triumph over my enemies was to destroy them, to carry out my Day of Retribution, to exact my ultimate and devastating vengeance against all of the popular young people who never accepted me and against all women for rejecting me and starving me of love and sex."

In the spring of 2013, Elliot expanded his arsenal by acquiring another deadly weapon: a Sig Sauer P226. Fueled by his growing rage and desperation, he attended a college party in hopes of finally losing his virginity. In the two weeks leading up to the event, he dedicated himself to working out, believing that two weeks of pumping iron would make him irresistible to women. Elliot was destined to be let down again.

Consumed by a mixture of alcohol, frustration, and a deep sense of entitlement, Elliot confronted an Asian man at the party who was engaged in conversation with a white girl. The mere sight of an Asian man interacting with a white girl ignited a wave of anger within him.

> "I always felt as if white girls thought less of me because I was half-Asian, but then I see this white girl at the party talking to a full-blooded Asian. I never had that kind of attention from a

> white girl! And white girls are the only girls I'm
> attracted to, especially the blondes. How could
> an ugly Asian attract the attention of a white
> girl, while a beautiful Eurasian like myself never
> had any attention from them?"

Elliot's distorted beliefs about what he thought women
desired led him to believe that arrogance and cockiness were
the traits that would attract them. In a drunken state, he
approached the couple at the party and unleashed a torrent
of screams and verbal abuse toward them. After briefly
leaving the scene, he returned and continued his outburst.
Frustrated and unable to control his anger, he went outside
and climbed onto a ten-foot ledge, isolating himself from the
crowd below.

Elliot observed the festivities from his vantage point, his
mind consumed by resentment and hatred. In a disturbing
gesture, he raised his arm, formed his fingers into the shape
of a gun, and pretended to shoot. He then stood and
screamed at other attendees nearby, specifically targeting
girls, and even made an attempt to push them off the ledge in
his growing rage. But instead of pushing them off, other boys
at the party ganged up on him and pushed him off the ledge.

> "I rose from my chair and tried to act arrogant
> and cocky toward them, throwing insults at
> everyone. They only laughed at me and started
> insulting me back. That was the last straw. I had
> taken enough insults that night. A dark, hate-
> fueled rage overcame my entire being, and I
> tried to push as many of them as I could from
> the 10-foot ledge. My main target was the girls. I

wanted to punish them for talking to the obnoxious boys instead of me."

The violent encounter on the ledge left Elliot with a shattered leg: a painful, physical reminder of the chaos and
hostility that had consumed him. Drunk and angry, he
hobbled away, nursing his injuries. However, amid his intoxication, Elliot realized he had dropped his Gucci sunglasses, a
gift from his mother.

Elliot went back to the area where he thought the incident
had occurred to retrieve his sunglasses. But he was too
drunk, and mistakenly went to the wrong house party. He
screamed at the partygoers to return his sunglasses, but they
had no idea what he was talking about. Several young men at
the party responded with aggression, pushing him down and
punching and kicking him. Injured and emotionally overwhelmed, Elliot made his way home, only to discover that he
had also lost his gold necklace during the scuffle.

During the early months of 2014, Elliot Rodger spent his
time driving through the scenic landscapes of Montecito and
Santa Barbara. He recorded videos for his YouTube channel,
where he reflected on his miserable existence and contem-
plated his twisted plan for retribution against humanity. In
these recordings, he arrogantly referred to himself as the
"Magnificent Gentleman," unable to comprehend why
women were not drawn to someone as "beautiful" and "magnificent" as he believed himself to be.

In May 2014, Elliot uploaded a video to YouTube expressing his deep despair and loneliness. Concerned for his well-being, his mother came across the video and became worried that he might be contemplating suicide. She decided to call the police for assistance. When the officers arrived and spoke to Elliot, he managed to convince them that he was "just fine," downplaying any thoughts of self-harm and assuring them that his online rants were harmless. Unbeknownst to them, hidden just a few feet away in his bedroom were three guns and a significant amount of ammunition, along with his extensive 107,000-word manifesto titled "My Twisted World: The Story of Elliot Rodger." Unaware of the dangerous arsenal within his reach, the officers left without further intervention, oblivious to the festering hatred in Elliot's disturbed mind.

———

On his planned "Day of Retribution," Elliot devised a horrifying sequence of events. His initial targets were to be his stepmother, Soumaya, and his younger brother, Jazz, whom he intended to kill while his father was away. He planned to return to Santa Barbara in his father's SUV and target his roommates, using their apartment as a trap to lure in more unsuspecting victims.

On the following day, Elliot's focus shifted to the Alpha Phi Sorority of the University of California at Santa Barbara. In his disturbed mind, this all-female dormitory, known for its attractive blonde residents, represented the epitome of beauty. There, he intended to unleash his violence and inflict unimaginable harm.

After murdering as many girls as he could at the sorority, he would then turn his attention to Del Playa Drive, a road running parallel to the Isla Vista coastline, where he intended to mow down as many unsuspecting victims as possible with his SUV. He would then take his own life with one of his three guns.

Elliot viewed himself as a deity worthy of more than mere human existence. He wrote,

> "I am Elliot Rodger, magnificent, glorious, supreme, eminent, divine. I am the closest thing there is to a living God. Humanity is a disgusting, depraved, and evil species. It is my purpose to punish them all. I will purify the world of everything that is wrong with it. On the Day of Retribution, I will truly be a powerful God, punishing everyone I deem to be impure and depraved."

———

But as the day approached, Elliot's father had a last-minute change of plans. He would not be out of town, which meant Elliot couldn't kill Soumaya and Jazz. Nor would he be able to use the family SUV. Instead, he resorted to using his own BMW.

The day before carrying out his plan, Elliot Rodger uploaded his final video to YouTube, where he ranted,

> "Well, this is my last video. It has all had to come to this. Tomorrow is the day of retribution, the day in which I will have my revenge against humanity. Against all of you. For the last eight years of my life, ever since I hit puberty, I've been forced to endure an existence of loneliness,

rejection, and unfulfilled desires, all because girls have never been attracted to me. Girls gave their affection, sex, and love to other men but never to me.

I'm 22 years old, and I'm still a virgin. I've never even kissed a girl. I've been through college for two and a half years—more than that, actually— and I'm still a virgin. It has been very torturous. College is the time when everyone experiences those things, such as sex, fun, and pleasure. Within those years, I've had to rot in loneliness. It's not fair.

You girls have never been attracted to me. I don't know why you girls aren't attracted to me, but I will punish you all for it. It's an injustice, a crime, because... I don't know what you don't see in me. I'm the perfect guy, and yet you throw yourselves at these obnoxious men instead of me, the supreme gentleman.

I will punish all of you for it. (laughs) On the Day of Retribution, I'm going to enter the hottest sorority house at UCSB. And I will slaughter every single spoiled, stuck-up, blonde slut I see inside there. All those girls I've desired so much, they would have all rejected me and looked down upon me as an inferior man if I ever made a sexual advance toward them (scoffs) while they throw themselves at these obnoxious brutes. I'll take great pleasure in slaughtering all of you.

You will finally see that I am, in truth, the supe-rior one. The true alpha male. (laughs) Yes. After

I've annihilated every single girl in the sorority house, I will take to the streets of Isla Vista and slay every single person I see there. All those popular kids who live such lives of hedonistic pleasures while I've had to rot in loneliness for all these years. They've all looked down upon me every time I tried to go out and join them. They've all treated me like a mouse.

Well, now I will be a god compared to you. You will all be animals. You are animals, and I will slaughter you like animals. And I will be a god. Exacting my retribution on all those who deserve it. You do deserve it, just for the crime of living a better life than me. All you popular kids, you've never accepted me, and now you will all pay for it. And girls, all I ever wanted was to love you and to be loved by you. I've wanted a girlfriend; I've wanted sex; I've wanted love, affection, adoration. You think I'm unworthy of it. That's a crime that can never be forgiven.

If I can't have you, girls, I will destroy you. (laughs) You denied me a happy life, and in turn, I will deny all of you life. (laughs) It's only fair.

I hate all of you. Humanity is a disgusting, wretched, depraved species. If I had it in my power, I would stop at nothing to reduce every single one of you to mountains of skulls and rivers of blood. And rightfully so. You deserve to be annihilated. And I'll give that to you. You never showed me any mercy, so I will show you none. (Laughs) You forced me to suffer all my life and now I will make you suffer. I've waited a long time for this. I'll give you exactly what you deserve. All of you. All of you girls who rejected me and looked down upon me, and you know, treated me like scum. While you gave yourselves to other men.

And all of you men, for living a better life than me, all of you sexually active men, I hate you. I hate all of you. I can't wait to give you exactly what you deserve. Utter annihilation."

————

The video was uploaded to YouTube at 9:17 PM on May 23, 2014. One minute after uploading the video, he emailed his 137-page manifesto to thirty-four people, including his parents, family members, therapist, former teachers, and childhood friends.

Elliot's therapist was the first to react and quickly called his mother. She called Elliot's father and the police, and they all raced to his apartment at 6598 Seville Road #7, but Elliot had already put his plan into motion. By the time she dialed 911, three people were already dead.

His first victims were three unsuspecting young men; George Chen, Chengyuan "James" Hong, and Weihan "David" Wang. Two had been his roommates, and another was a friend. They had been slaughtered separately throughout the day as they entered the apartment. The brutal attack left the three bodies with a total of 142 stab wounds. When the police arrived, they found a bloody towel, indicating that Elliot had feebly attempted to clean up the blood, but there was just too much of it. Elliot, however, had fled.

Elliot had killed the three men before he uploaded the video and emailed the manifesto. After the stabbing, he purchased coffee at Starbucks, drove to the Alpha Phi sorority house at 840 Embarcadero Del Norte, and pounded on the front door repeatedly, but he got no answer. Frustrated, he retreated back onto the street and shot at the first targets he encountered. Three young women belonging to the Delta Delta Delta sorority were shot. Katherine Breann Cooper and Veronica Elizabeth Weiss were killed instantly, while Bianca de Kock was injured.

Rodger quickly fled the scene in his BMW and drove down Pardall Road, firing into buildings and hoping to hit an innocent victim. Luckily, the first building, a coffee shop, was closed and unoccupied. However, further down Pardall Road, Christopher Michaels-Martinez stood outside Isla Vista Deli Mart when Rodger stopped his car briefly, got out, and started shooting. Michaels-Martinez was shot seven times and died at the scene.

On the streets of Isla Vista, Elliot Rodger's violent rampage came to a tragic and devastating end. Despite the efforts of law enforcement to apprehend him and put a stop to his horrifying acts, Elliot continued his assault on innocent pedestrians, shooting and intentionally striking them with his vehicle. The pursuit by sheriff's deputies only escalated the situation, with Elliot firing back at them in a desperate attempt to evade capture.

As the chase climaxed near the intersection of El Embarcadero and Sabato Tarde, Elliot sustained a gunshot wound to the hip but continued to drive recklessly. He then deliberately struck a man on a bicycle as he turned onto Del Playa. Knowing the inevitable outcome, Elliot decided to take his own life. He turned his gun on himself while still driving.

The impact of the crash brought his BMW to a halt, marking the end of the tragic and violent spree.

———

The aftermath of Elliot Rodger's attack in Isla Vista was a scene of unimaginable horror and devastation. When officers discovered him in his car at 9:35 p.m., it became evident how extensively-planned and deadly his attack had been. Inside the BMW were three pistols, several blood-covered hunting knives, six empty ten-round magazines, and a staggering 548 unspent rounds of ammunition.

Elliot's violent actions resulted in the loss of six innocent lives. Three people died from stab wounds, and three others died from gunfire. The impact of his spree extended beyond those who lost their lives, as fourteen victims survived the attack but were left traumatized and injured. Among the survivors, seven had sustained gunshot wounds, while the remaining seven had been struck by Elliot's vehicle.

———

The following day, a candlelight memorial was held to honor the victims, who will forever be remembered for their academic talents, volunteer work, and loving natures.

In the aftermath of the devastating massacre, a memorial service was held at UC Santa Barbara's Harder Stadium, where over 20,000 people gathered to pay their respects to the fallen. Elliot Rodger's father, Peter, made a heartbreaking appearance on television, expressing his anger, despair, and confusion over his son's actions. He candidly admitted that, at times, the pain caused by Elliot was so overwhelming that he wished his son had never been born. The emotional toll of the tragedy was palpable as the community struggled to come to terms with the loss of so many young lives.

———

Elliot Rodger soon gained infamy as the "King of the Incels" (involuntary celibates) among a group of individuals who lamented their lack of romantic or sexual relationships, despite wanting them. In this online community, Rodger found comfort in the idea that his struggles were understood and even accepted. But to the vast majority, Rodger was defined as a misogynistic, racist, and narcissistic monster with a deep-seated hatred for women and self-proclaimed superiority over people of other races and ethnicities.

CHAPTER 9
TOUCHDOWNS AND POM-POMS

One fall evening in 2014, the spotlight fell on a new addition to the cheerleading team at Knoxville, Tennessee's Central High School. Fourteen-year-old Emma Walker stood out as the sole freshman to secure a spot on the team that year. Her passion, spirit, and infectious smile quickly became her defining features as she threw herself wholeheartedly into the world of cheerleading.

Being in that lively environment brought immense joy to Emma's life. Known for her kind and caring nature, she was always there to support her teammates and uplift their spirits. Alongside her cheerleading aspirations, Emma nurtured dreams of pursuing a career as a neonatal nurse, driven by her desire to provide compassionate care to sick or premature newborn babies.

As fate would have it, one evening, while Emma was on the sidelines showing off her cheerleading skills, she captured the attention of Riley Gaul, the star wide receiver for the school's football team.

Riley saw Emma, with her short skirt and her pom-poms, and at that moment, an undeniable spark ignited between them. He was in his senior year, while she was just a four-teen-year-old freshman, but despite their two-year age difference, they immediately hit it off.

Riley was a talented athlete, a standout student, and a well-liked figure at the school. In addition to his achievements on the football field, he actively participated in the local church, harbored a love for video games, and was known among his friends for his playful nature. He defied the stereotype of a typical jock, possessing a unique charm that resonated with those around him.

Although Riley was already in a relationship when he met Emma, their connection grew stronger by the day, eventually prompting him to make a difficult decision. With sincerity and honesty, Riley ended his previous relationship to pursue a romantic journey with Emma.

As the football star and cheerleader, Riley and Emma embodied the quintessential popular high school couple. Their relationship blossomed, with their magnetic connection evident to all who knew them.

Right away, Riley seamlessly integrated himself into Emma's family, leaving a positive impression on her parents. They regarded him as the epitome of the boy next door—polite, well-mannered, and inherently likable. However, their initial fondness for Riley began to waver when they discovered an unsettling truth.

News reached Emma's parents that Riley had made a promise to his ex-girlfriend to take her to her junior prom. However, he also intended to take Emma to his senior prom. Riley's action damaged Emma's parents' perception of him.

The once-warm feelings toward him transformed into disappointment and raised questions about his integrity and commitment.

Despite her parents' concerns, Emma appeared unfazed by the prom arrangement. She knew her relationship with Riley was strong. Her social media accounts were a testament to their connection, as they overflowed with snapshots of the young couple. Affectionate pictures and playful selfies showcased their shared moments and deep caring for one another.

While Emma's friends observed her happiness from their photos, they admitted to finding it challenging to get to know Riley. They thought that the fact that he was quiet and seemed shy was why it was hard to get along with him. Emma's friends, while remaining supportive, believed that Riley was just introverted and cautious when it came to forming new relationships.

Amidst the differences of opinion, Emma remained steadfast in her faith in Riley, hoping that time would help bridge the gap between him and her loved ones. She believed that beneath his reserved exterior lay a genuine and caring person worthy of the trust and acceptance she had placed in him.

———

But as time passed, Emma's friends started to see a different side of Riley. They initially tried to excuse his actions by blaming his shyness. However, as more incidents occurred, their worries grew stronger and outweighed any prior justifications.

Her friends became increasingly aware of Riley's desire to keep Emma from associating with anyone besides himself.

He showed signs of possessiveness, a worrying level of jealousy, and controlling tendencies.

Emma's friends voiced concerns regarding the unhealthy dynamics in her relationship. She needed to be made aware of the potential harm these actions could cause. Emma, on the other hand, downplayed their worries, insinuating that there was nothing to be concerned about and defending every move Riley made.

―――――

Emma's parents took a drastic step to protect her because they knew how toxic her relationship had become. To stop the unhealthy communication, they decided to confiscate her phone. Riley, however, was resourceful; he gave Emma an iPod Touch so she could secretly use Wi-Fi to talk to him without her parents knowing. This covert communication highlighted how much Riley had influenced Emma's life.

―――――

Over the next two years, Emma and Riley's relationship spiraled into a tumultuous cycle of getting together and breaking up repeatedly. The tension in their relationship only got worse over time.

Each breakup became more dramatic and was accompanied by bitter arguments. Riley's actions became increasingly out of control, to the point where he constantly bombarded her with calls and text messages. He went to great lengths, waiting for hours outside her workplace until her shift ended. On multiple occasions, he sent hurtful text messages,

> "You're dead to me. I'll check the obituary. Fuck you."

> "I hate you. I hate everything about you. You're the biggest bitch I've ever come into contact with."

But for every hurtful message or cruel action, Riley quickly followed up with an apology. He expressed remorse, stating, "I'm sorry for however I act. I love you more than words can describe." These intermittent apologies created a cycle of hope and manipulation, making it challenging for Emma to break free from the unhealthy relationship.

During this volatile period, Emma's parents, Mark and Jill, tried to persuade her to end the relationship. They recognized his destructive nature and understood the importance of their daughter's well-being. Mark and Jill fervently hoped that Emma would find the strength to sever ties with Riley and escape the cycle of instability that had engulfed her life.

———

Conflicts in the family grew due to Emma's parents' persistent attempts to persuade her to end the relationship. Tensions rose as Emma's deep emotional attachment to Riley clashed with their advice.

Emma and Riley's relationship was still on and off in the fall of 2016. Riley had just finished high school and was starting his first year at Maryville College, about 30 minutes away. At the same time, Emma began her junior year of high school when she was 16.

Even though they lived in different places, it didn't do much to change the toxic patterns that plagued their relationship.

Those who cared about her were filled with worry because the same patterns of control, possessiveness, and emotional instability repeated themselves.

Just before Halloween of that year, Emma's parents made a tough choice in an effort to safeguard their daughter. They took severe action by grounding her and only letting her leave the house for school and cheerleading-related activities. They also assumed the duty of closely monitoring her movements and the people she encountered. Surprisingly, the increased vigilance seemed to pay off, giving them cause for cautious optimism.

When Emma's father, Mark, witnessed the change in his daughter, he remarked, "She was like her old self again." Because there were fewer influences and distractions from the outside world, Emma was able to start rebuilding her relationship with her family. She enthusiastically participated in the family's activities, including interacting with other people and eating family dinners together.

The news that Emma had decided to stop her connection with Riley sent a wave of relief to her friends. The idea that Emma had finally cut ties with the toxic relationship gave them hope. However, Riley's response to the separation was quite different from what they had imagined.

————

Emma's parents gave her permission to go to a party at a friend's home on Friday, November 18, 2016. As the evening wore on, her friend Zach showed up at the party at around 11:30 p.m. Emma pulled him inside with a feeling of urgency. She told Zach she was upset and worried because

she was getting strange text messages from a number she
didn't know.

Emma showed Zach one of the messages, which read,

> "Come outside alone if you don't want to see a
> loved one get hurt. Go to your car with your
> keys. If you don't comply, I will hurt them."

Emma was alarmed and nervous, but she suspected it was one of
Riley's friends pulling a sophisticated practical joke on her. She
reacted stubbornly by threatening to contact the police to stop
the upsetting communications. However, that caution didn't
stop the sender, and the messages' content only worsened.

Then, amid the exchanges, Emma received another message
that filled her with dread. It said that Riley had been dumped
from a car outside the house.

Emma and Zach reacted quickly and rushed outside, where
they discovered Riley face down in a nearby ditch. Riley
appeared confused and cradled his head in apparent disori-
entation. He claimed he was abducted, though he had no clue
how he arrived there.

Emma was overcome with emotion as she reiterated to Riley
that they had broken up. She urged him to respect her decision and leave her alone. Riley walked away from the scene,
alone and despondent, down the street. In a state of distress,
he reached out to his friend Noah and informed him that he
had been abducted. Noah, on the other hand, knew Riley
well and had a hard time believing his elaborate story.

The event left Emma with a lingering sense of unease and
concern, and she chose to stay the night with her friends. Just

after ten the following morning, Emma returned to her house with her friend Haley, who also lived nearby. As they got close to their homes, they saw a suspicious-looking male figure clad in all black wandering down the street. Emma took Haley home and returned to her own house, but she knew something was wrong.

Emma began getting dressed with the intention of seeing her mother, Jill, soon after. However, her calm was suddenly disturbed when the mysterious black-clad man appeared again, and he began repeatedly ringing the doorbell and pounding on the door. Emma was in a panic and sent frantic texts to her friends in an effort to get assistance.

> "I'm home alone and somebody in all black walked down my street and came to my door and rang the doorbell over and over again. I thought I was going to die."

Despite their tumultuous past, she also reached out to the one person she knew would come to save her: Riley. Her message read,

> "I hate you, but I need you right now."

Emma received a prompt response from Riley, who reassured her that he was on his way to save her.

When Riley arrived, the mysterious man miraculously disappeared. Emma's friend Haley was sure it was Riley, especially after seeing his car parked down the street. She even texted Riley about his presence, but he denied it.

Emma's mother, Jill Walker, returned home and found Emma and Riley talking in the front yard. Jill reminded Riley that he wasn't allowed near the house and ordered him to leave. Emma was visibly shaken, concerned that the man pounding on the door may have been a burglar. Jill, however, suspected it was more than a coincidence. Emma reassured her mother that Riley had nothing to do with the incident, but Jill knew her daughter was being naive.

Jill and Mark, deeply worried for their daughter's safety, accompanied Emma to her Sunday morning shift at work, waited for her to finish, and drove her back home after her shift.

———

On Sunday, November 20, 2016, as darkness fell, there was calmness throughout the Walker home. Before going to bed at midnight, Emma spoke with her friend Keegan about an upcoming school assignment. Riley, who was back in Maryville, asked to use his roommate's phone just after midnight and called Emma. Emma told him in no uncertain terms that she didn't want to get back together with him, then cut the conversation short. He bombarded her with texts and made over forty phone calls, leaving repeated messages on her voicemail. However, frustrated and tired, Emma muted her phone and went to sleep.

———

The sounds that appeared to be coming from within the home and a door slamming twice woke Emma's father that night. He got up and peeked into Emma's bedroom, as well as the bedroom of her brother, Evan, but everything seemed fine. Assuming the noises were part of a dream, he returned to bed.

At 6 a.m., Jill entered Emma's room to wake her up for school. Despite calling out her name, Emma didn't move. Concerned, Jill reached out and touched her daughter's leg, but when she felt the chill of her skin, Jill involuntarily snapped her hand back in shock. Peering at Emma's face, she realized something was gravely wrong. Without hesitation, Jill grabbed the telephone and called 911.

Emma's complexion was pale, and her lips had taken on a troubling shade of blue. Frantically, Jill searched for a pulse, but it was no use. When emergency crews arrived, it was determined Emma had been dead for several hours.

———

Police arrived to a distressing scene in Emma's bedroom. A small amount of blood near her mouth hinted at the possibility of vomiting, suggesting she may have ingested something harmful. However, upon closer inspection, the police discovered an unexpected detail—a small hole in the wall of Emma's bedroom. This shifted their focus. Investigators then realized that someone had fired a bullet through the wall, striking Emma in the head while she slept.

As the investigation unfolded, authorities came across two shell casings outside the home, indicating that two shots had been fired. Determined to trace the trajectory of the second shot, the police meticulously surveyed the perimeter of the residence. Eventually, their search led them to discover another bullet hole situated at a similar height to the first.

The investigation revealed that the second shot had been fired into Emma's bedroom, near her bed. The evidence indicated that the gunshots had been discharged from a distance of only four or five feet from her bedroom window. The medical examiner determined she had died somewhere between 2:30 and 3:00 a.m.

One of the bullets struck Emma behind her left ear, killing her instantly. The second bullet was found embedded in her pillow, narrowly missing her. The precision of the shots suggested that the shooter possessed intimate knowledge of the room's layout and was aware of Emma's sleeping position. Investigators came to the chilling conclusion that Emma's circumstances were known to the person who committed this deliberate and calculated act of violence.

A candlelight vigil was held at Central High School to remember Emma. Friends, family, and community members came to pay their respects. At the football game that week, Emma's fellow cheerleaders released balloons into the sky as a touching way to remember her. After Emma Walker's untimely death, the community was filled with heartfelt tributes. Riley Gaul, Emma's ex-boyfriend, sent his condolences.

Authorities began their investigation by questioning Emma's close contacts. One name kept coming up during these conversations: Riley Gaul. As the investigation into Emma's death progressed, it became clear that Riley had played a pivotal role in her life. This led the police to concentrate their attention on him.

Riley Gaul's friends were concerned about his mental health after Emma's murder and voiced their concerns to the police. During questioning, several of Riley's friends told detectives a secret he had told them the day after he said he was abducted.

According to their statements, Riley claimed he was terrified and feared his life was in danger. He told them he had stolen his grandfather's gun to protect himself. Riley had shown the pistol to one of his friends, Alex.

Riley contacted another acquaintance, Noah, and asked for advice on removing fingerprints from a handgun. He claimed the request was on his roommate's behalf, but investigators believed it could be a sign that he was trying to hide his connection with the gun.

In the days leading up to the shooting of Emma, Riley's grandfather filed a theft report on the same firearm that Riley had displayed to his friends.

Feeling the weight of the situation, Riley asked his friends Noah and Alex for assistance in getting rid of the gun in the Tennessee River. Riley stated he was concerned that the pistol might somehow incriminate him in Emma's murder, although he insisted he had nothing to do with it.

Realizing the seriousness of the situation, investigators brought Riley in for questioning. He steadfastly denied having a gun and said he would never harm Emma. Yet investigators detected something odd about his manner. Riley seemed detached and emotionless. What was stranger, though, was that he couldn't manage to speak Emma's name and referred to her as "the girl."

> Riley: "The girl... She, uh, she texted me."
>
> Detective: "Which girl?"
>
> Riley: "The one that passed away."
>
> Detective: "Okay, what's her name?"
>
> Riley: "Emma."

The investigators resumed their questioning. They interrogated him about the stolen pistol and the comments made by Noah and Alex, who had told police about his request for help getting rid of the gun. Riley, however, denied ever having such talks or being involved in the events leading up to Emma's death.

As the investigation continued, detectives learned critical facts about Riley Gaul's cell phone activity. Even though he lived in Maryville, the data showed that his phone had connected to a cell tower near Emma's house in Knoxville at 3:45 a.m. This digital trail proved that Riley was close to Emma's home between 2:30 and 3:00 a.m., when she was believed to have been killed.

———

Riley was the primary suspect in the investigation, but they didn't have enough evidence to arrest him. After leaving the police station, Riley sent text messages to Noah and Alex, advising them to erase their texts and cautioning them against ever speaking to the police again.

He had no idea that Alex and Noah had been working with the police. The young men were devoted to aiding the investigation and had confidence in their ability to retrieve the murder weapon. At first, the police warned them against becoming involved because of the dangers involved. However, Alex and Noah emphasized their desire to do the right thing despite the hazards. They remained steadfast and committed to supporting the investigation.

Noah and Alex devised a plan with the police to expose Riley's lies. They agreed to assist Riley in disposing of the gun in the Tennessee River. The police would be stationed nearby, prepared to apprehend Riley when he revealed the weapon. The boys were given code words to text the police, indicating the right moment for them to intervene. Equipped with wires and body cameras provided by the investigation team, a complex undercover operation began.

The three young men headed to the river with the gun from Riley's grandfather's house. Once there, Riley pulled out the weapon to dispose of it, unaware that the police were prepared. Thanks to Noah and Alex's cooperation, officers were waiting, and Riley Gaul was taken into custody. Just forty-eight hours after Emma's death, Riley Gaul was arrested and charged with murder.

———

Police discovered black clothing and shoes in the trunk of Riley's car, leading them to conclude that he was the individual terrorizing Emma at her home a few days earlier.

During Riley Gaul's trial, which began a year and a half later, he pleaded not guilty and opted not to testify on his own behalf. His defense team chose not to present any witnesses.

Instead of contesting his role, their approach centered on claiming that the gunshot was a careless mistake. They argued that Riley was shooting near Emma to startle her, not realizing the bullets would pass through the wall. They claimed that he only wanted to win her trust and restart their romance.

According to his lawyer, Emma viewed Riley as her hero, and the ill-conceived plan was an attempt to stage a rescue that tragically resulted in her accidental death. The defense urged the jury that, if they found Riley guilty, to consider reckless homicide, which carried a significantly lesser penalty.

The prosecution argued, however, that Riley shot Emma deliberately out of resentment that she had rejected his attempts at reconciliation.

Prosecutors accused Riley of fabricating a false kidnapping story to distress Emma. He then highlighted the alarming circumstances of the defendant being outside a sixteen-year-old girl's bedroom in the early morning, dressed in black. He questioned why the defendant chose to shoot at that specific location, suggesting that the shot placement indicated an intent to kill rather than other available options.

The jury found William Riley Gaul guilty of first-degree murder in the shooting death of Emma Walker, as well as charges of stalking, theft, reckless endangerment, and firearm possession during a violent crime.

In Tennessee, a first-degree murder conviction carries an automatic life sentence, meaning he will spend the remainder of his days behind bars. Riley Gaul will be in his 70s by the time he has the opportunity for parole.

Riley Gaul requested an acquittal in May 2021, arguing that the evidence was inadequate. He sought a second trial if the acquittal was not given. On June 4, 2021, a motion hearing was planned. However, his request was eventually turned down. Riley's lawyer said that they planned to appeal the decision.

Emma, who was due to graduate in May 2018, was never given the chance to do so. Her cap and gown were tastefully set on the chair designated for her, and despite her absence, her family accepted her diploma on her behalf.

After Emma's death, her loved ones have worked hard to preserve her memory. Her high school has created a scholarship in her honor as evidence of her ongoing influence.

Jill spoke about how Emma's love of animals and desire to work as a neonatal nurse were fundamental parts of who she was. The Walker family has made significant gifts in honor of her interests. They successfully added Emma's name to a dog park and a patient room in the East Tennessee Children's Hospital neonatal critical care unit.

CHAPTER 10
THE REVOLVING DOORS

Born in Mound City, Missouri, on July 16, 1929, Charles Ray Hatcher was doomed to live a life marred by bloodshed and despair. The instability in his childhood home life paved the way for his future troubles.

Hatcher, the youngest of Jesse James and Lula Novada Hatcher's four children, grew up in a small village outside St. Joseph, Missouri. Sadly, the instability he brought into their home was a direct result of his father, who was a bootlegger and abusive alcoholic. As a child, Charles bore the brunt of his father's abuse and violence, which left scars that would influence his future path in life.

School proved to be no refuge for Hatcher. He became a target of bullying, which only fueled his tendencies toward aggression. Rather than seeking solace, he lashed out at his classmates, establishing a pattern of intimidation that would persist into his adult life.

Tragedy struck Charles Hatcher's life in the spring of 1936, when a seemingly innocent childhood activity turned fatal. While flying a kite with his brother, they unknowingly used copper wire they had found in an old Model T Ford. Tragically, just as Hatcher's older brother, Arthur Allen, was about to hand him the kite, it made contact with a high-voltage power line, electrocuting Arthur on the spot. The loss of his brother was a devastating blow, further fracturing an already-fragile family dynamic.

In the aftermath of the tragedy, Hatcher's father abandoned the family, leaving his mother, Lula, to navigate the challenges of single motherhood. Lula remarried multiple times in search of stability, and in 1945, Hatcher and his mother relocated to St. Joseph, hoping for a fresh start.

The transfer to St. Joseph provided little change for Hatcher. He carried the emotional scars of his past and retained hatred and contempt. His burgeoning dark inclinations were further fueled by the new environment's inability to provide him with the stability he so badly wanted.

The stage was set for Hatcher as a young man scarred by a turbulent childhood and plagued by unresolved trauma. As he entered adulthood, the demons within him began to stir, signaling the emergence of a cold and remorseless predator.

———

Charles Ray Hatcher's life was a revolving door of crime and punishment, with each incarceration fueling the darkness within him. In 1947, he was convicted of stealing a logging truck from his employer and received a suspended sentence. The following year, he stole a Buick and was sentenced to two years in prison.

Released from prison on June 8, 1949, after serving a little over half of his sentence for auto theft, it didn't take long for Hatcher to find himself behind bars once again.

In a matter of months, Hatcher's desperation led him to commit forgery, attempting to cash a counterfeit $10 check at a gas station in Maryville, Missouri. The law caught up with him, but on March 18, 1951, he escaped and attempted another burglary. He was quickly apprehended and found himself back within prison walls, serving an extra two years for his crimes.

But prison seemed to have little impact on Hatcher's trajectory. On July 14, 1954, he was released again, only to steal a 1951 Ford in Orrick, Missouri, shortly afterward. This act landed him another four-year sentence, further solidifying his status as a repeat offender. Not one to let an opportunity slip away, Hatcher attempted to escape from the Ray County Jail in Richmond before his sentencing, earning himself an additional two years behind bars.

Hatcher was released from jail for the sixth time on March 18, 1959, but it was obvious that freedom only enticed him down an even darker road. He still had an unquenchable hunger for mayhem, and his criminal impulses were unaffected.

On June 26, 1959, Hatcher targeted Steven Pellham, a 16-year-old newspaper delivery boy in St. Joseph, raising the bar for his depravity. Hatcher attempted to kidnap the unaware adolescent while brandishing a butcher knife. Thankfully, Pellham was able to flee and quickly informed the police of the incident. Shortly afterward, Charles Hatcher was stopped by the police while operating a stolen car, ending his reign of terror.

Hatcher received a five-year term in the Missouri State Prison for attempted kidnapping and vehicle theft after the legal system passed the Habitual Criminal Act. Hatcher tried to escape from the Buchanan County Prison as he was being transported to jail, revealing his crafty side once again. Local publications described him as the most infamous criminal in northwest Missouri since Jesse James.

Charles Ray Hatcher didn't waste time leaving a deadly legacy after arriving at Missouri State Prison. On July 2, 1961, the motionless corpse of a twenty-six-year-old prisoner named Jerry Tharrington was found on the floor of the kitchen loading dock, having been viciously raped and fatally stabbed several times. Hatcher was the only person on the kitchen staff who was missing at the time of the murder. Therefore, all the evidence pointed squarely to him. The courts, however, were unable to convict him of killing Tharrington. Instead, he was placed in solitary confinement.

Hatcher tried to take advantage of the system when he was being held in isolation. He faked the need for mental health therapy in a letter, expecting it to be his way out of seclusion and possibly lead to an early release. Nevertheless, the jail psychologist could see through his charade and dismissed it as a sham. Hatcher was sent to the general jail population after his plea for therapy was ruled down.

Hatcher's sentence was ultimately reduced to three-quarters of the initial amount of time, resulting in his release on August 24, 1963, despite the murder allegation hanging over his head.

———

Six years after his release, on August 27, 1969, Charles Hatcher kidnapped 12-year-old William Freeman in Antioch, California, as he rode his bicycle. He enticed the young boy to a stream, where he tortured and murdered him by strangling him, taking a life full of promise and innocence.

Six-year-old Gilbert Martinez was reported missing two days later in San Francisco, just forty-five miles away. The boy had been playing with a small girl who said he had walked off with a stranger who offered him ice cream.

Thankfully, a man walking his dog intervened when he witnessed the assailant sexually assaulting and physically beating the defenseless child. The attacker was apprehended by the police, providing the false name of Albert Ralph Price despite carrying identification bearing the name Horace Prater. He remained uncooperative during questioning, refusing to reveal his true identity—Charles Ray Hatcher.

Masquerading as Albert Price, Hatcher faced charges of assault with an attempt to commit sodomy and kidnapping. However, his mental state raised concerns about his competency to stand trial. Competency evaluations were ordered, but Hatcher remained unresponsive during the preliminary assessments. He pretended to hear voices and feigned delusions and suicide attempts in a calculated effort to avoid facing the consequences of his actions.

Eventually, FBI agents positively identified him as Charles Ray Hatcher.

In December 1970, Hatcher became a pawn in a back-and-forth game between the courts and various hospitals. Psychiatric evaluations offered conflicting insights into his mental condition. One psychiatrist diagnosed him with a passive-aggressive personality, along with paraphilia and pedophilia tendencies. However, hospital staff grew skeptical, believing that Hatcher was fabricating or exaggerating his symptoms.

In January of 1971, he was evaluated by two more psychiatrists. One concluded that he was insane and recommended receiving intensive treatment in a secure facility, while the other concluded that he was incompetent to stand trial and sent him back to the hospital.

The judicial processes surrounding Hatcher's case continued for some time, culminating in a trial on May 24, 1971. Hatcher entered a not-guilty plea on the grounds of insanity. He was ordered to undergo further testing after being found unfit to stand trial. Hatcher did manage to flee the hospital on June 2, but his freedom was brief. Under the guise of Richard Lee Grady, he was captured in Colusa, California, a week later on suspicion of vehicle theft.

After Hatcher was apprehended, the California State Hospital received him again for a psychiatric assessment. He was sent to the prison state hospital in Vacaville in April 1972 after it was determined that his therapy had been unsuccessful and that he posed a risk to other patients.

He was sent to San Quentin State Prison in August 1972, three years after the horrific assault of Gilbert Martinez, to finally stand trial. One of two final examinations was used to determine his ability to stand trial, and the other was used to assess his mental state at the time of the crime.

———

In December 1972, Hatcher stood trial for the abduction and molestation of Martinez. He was eventually convicted and committed to the California State Hospital as a "mentally disordered sexual offender" in January 1973. However, Hatcher's insidious nature refused to be contained.

On March 28, 1973, security guards found Hatcher hiding in a cooler near the central courtyard of the hospital. He had two sheets stuffed into his pants, which showed that he was planning to escape. He was brought back to court to be sentenced after admitting he was complicit in the plot. The doctors decided he needed more containment because he was still a threat to society.

Hatcher got a one-year-to-life sentence in April and was sent to a medium-security prison in Vacaville. As time passed, psychologists dug deeper into Hatcher's twisted mind and found that he was a "manipulative institutionalized sociopath."

When he realized he would be moved to a maximum-security prison in June 1973, he cut his wrists in an attempt to kill himself. Another psychiatrist then diagnosed him with paranoid schizophrenia, which allowed him to stay in Vacaville medium-security prison.

Surprisingly, by August 1975, Hatcher's behavior in prison seemed to be getting better, and he got good reviews when he was reviewed for parole. The California Parole Board saw that he was making progress and gave him a parole date of December 25, 1978. But before he was released, there was a change in the law that gave credit for time spent in jails and mental hospitals; Hatcher was instead released earlier, in January 1977.

―――――

Hatcher's release from jail and his subsequent placement in a San Francisco halfway home, marked the beginning of yet another tumultuous period in his life. Eager to resume his malicious ways, Hatcher walked out as the doors opened.

————

The dark shadows cast by Charles Ray Hatcher's acts continued to grow longer, and as a result, more and more innocent lives were ruined. The horrifying circumstances surrounding the false conviction of an innocent man as a result of Hatcher's web of deceit may be seen in the case of Eric Christgen, who was only four years old at the time.

Just a year after Hatcher's most recent release, young Eric Christgen disappeared from downtown St. Joseph, Missouri, on May 26, 1978, shocking and terrifying the neighborhood. Sadly, his lifeless body was found along the banks of the Missouri River. The helpless youngster had endured an unspeakable sexual assault and was cruelly killed by asphyxia.

The thorough investigation that followed examined more than 100 probable suspects, including those with a history of antisocial conduct. The police interviewed "every known pervert in town," casting a broad net, but their efforts were fruitless. They were forced down a dangerous road by their urgent hunt for answers.

Melvin Reynolds, a twenty-five-year-old man with low intel-ligence, was caught in the investigation's net. Reynolds had personally experienced childhood sexual abuse and adoles-cent gay encounters. Suspicions clung to him despite his cooperation and readiness to undergo several interrogations, including hypnosis and polygraph tests. Reynolds was ques-tioned while under the influence of amobarbital, a purported truth serum, in December 1978.

Two months later, in February 1979, after being subjected to an arduous fourteen-hour interrogation filled with questions, promises, and threats, Reynolds finally succumbed. Overwhelmed and coerced, he uttered the words the authorities wanted to hear: "I'll say so if you want me to." The pressure he endured had taken its toll.

In the ensuing weeks, Reynolds embellished his confession with details that may or may not have been planted in his vulnerable mind under the weight of external influences and suggestions. This revised narrative proved convincing enough for the prosecutor to press charges against Reynolds. Eventually, a jury found him guilty of second-degree murder and sentenced him to life imprisonment.

———

The sound of Charles Ray Hatcher's footsteps reverberated over the countryside as his twisted path of murder claimed more lives. Using the alias Richard Clark, Hatcher was arrested in Omaha, Nebraska, on September 4, 1978, for the sexual assault of a 16-year-old child. The law mandated his commitment to the Douglas County Psychiatric Hospital. However, his time there was brief, and he was released after only four months.

Tragically, the freedom he gained would only lead to more suffering. Four months later, on May 3, 1979, Hatcher was arrested again for assault and attempted murder. His target was a seven-year-old boy named Thomas Morton, whom he tried to stab. The charges against Hatcher were dropped, but he was subsequently sent to the Norfolk Regional Center, a mental health facility, for evaluation and treatment.

Charles Ray Hatcher was released from the Norfolk Regional Center barely a year later, in May 1980. Unfortunately, his aggressive inclinations reappeared two months later, leading to another attack. He went back to the institution as a result. Hatcher escaped in September, but his thirst for mayhem was unquenchable.

Using the identity of Richard Clark once again, he was captured in Lincoln, Nebraska, on October 9, 1980. This time, he was accused of sodomizing and attempting to abuse a 17-year-old boy. He was sent to a different mental health hospital after his arrest. Amazingly, he was freed after just 21 days, leading many to doubt the efficacy of the system designed to save the defenseless.

Hatcher's unrelenting spiral of violence would continue in 1981. After a knife fight, he was apprehended once again on January 13 while posing as Richard Clark, this time in Des Moines, Iowa. As a result of his activities, he was admitted to several mental health institutions while the authorities tried to deal with his troubled condition. Hatcher was released to a Davenport Salvation Army shelter in April of the same year, after receiving treatment and being assessed.

It seemed that wherever he was sent, nobody wanted to keep Charles Ray Hatcher. His life was defined by multiple arrests, stints in mental health institutions, and brief periods of freedom after being released from such facilities. The issue remained: how much longer could society continue to put up with the existence of this lethal predator?

———

July 29, 1982, marked a somber day in St. Joseph as 11-year-old Michelle Steele was reported missing, sending shockwaves of fear and despair through the community. Tragically, her uncle found her body lifeless and brutalized on the Missouri River's banks the following day. Michelle had suffered the horrors of a brutal assault, having been beaten and strangled to death.

The investigation swiftly led authorities to a chilling discovery. The day after Michelle's body was found, Charles Ray Hatcher was apprehended and charged with murder as he attempted to check in at the St. Joseph State Hospital.

As Hatcher awaited trial for Michelle's murder, he shocked investigators with a staggering revelation. He confessed to fifteen additional murders dating back to 1969. One was that of Eric Christgen.

———

Four years after Melvin Reynolds was sentenced to life in prison, in a stunning turn of events, Charles Ray Hatcher confessed to the murder of Eric Christgen and two other victims in the presence of FBI agents. The veil of deception unraveled, exposing the injustice that had befallen Melvin Reynolds.

With Hatcher's admission, Reynolds was exonerated and regained his freedom. The revelation of Hatcher's guilt shed light on the manipulative tactics employed during Reynolds' interrogation, painting a disturbing picture of the lengths some members of law enforcement would go to in order to secure a conviction.

———

Among Hatcher's confessed crimes, he implicated himself in the abduction and murder of 12-year-old William Freeman, who had disappeared from Antioch, California, in August 1969, just a day before Hatcher faced child molestation charges in nearby San Francisco.

In a separate instance, Hatcher provided investigators with a crudely-drawn map that led them to the remains of 28-year-old James Churchill, buried on the Rock Island Army Arsenal grounds near Davenport, Iowa. During this time, Hatcher also confessed to the heinous murder of young Eric Christgen.

In October 1983, Hatcher was convicted of the Eric Christgen homicide, resulting in a life sentence with no possibility of parole for at least 50 years. The following year, facing his second Missouri conviction for the murder of Michelle Steele, Hatcher shockingly requested a death sentence. However, the jury refused his request, recommending a life term on December 3, 1984.

Just four days later, Hatcher succumbed to his demons and took his own life by hanging himself in his cell at the Missouri State Penitentiary in Jefferson City.

CHAPTER 11
TWISTED TRIANGLE

The first time Karen Hetrick and Kraig Kahler were introduced to one another was in 1983, when Karen was a first-year student at Kansas State University. Kraig was an exceptional student in the third year of his engineering program. He ranked first in his class and was successful in almost every endeavor he attempted. Karen and Kraig hit it off from the moment they first met, and within a few short weeks, they were head over heels in love with one another.

Both of them were smart and driven, and they had a wide variety of interests in common with one another. Their circle of friends believed that they were the pair that other people should strive to emulate, and they were positive that they would reach the pinnacle of their respective fields.

Once Kraig graduated from college, he was offered a promising position in Colorado almost immediately after. As a result, Karen decided to abandon her education, and the pair were married before starting their new life together in

Colorado. Not long after, Karen discovered she was pregnant with the couple's first child, Emily.

Over the years that followed, Karen and Kraig were the perfect example of a model marriage. They welcomed two more children into the world who they named Lauren and Sean, bought a wonderful home, and had a healthy relationship with one another.

In 1999, by which point Karen and Kraig had been married for seventeen years, he was offered a prestigious position with the city of Weatherford, Texas, as the Director of Utilities. It was an opportunity they couldn't turn down, since it came with a substantial pay raise.

Weatherford, a suburb west of Fort Worth, was a perfect fit for Karen, Kraig, and their family. He excelled at his new job, while Karen became president of the Local Mom's Group, and the two girls started an all-girl rock band with their friend, Cheyney. Kraig spent his free time playing baseball, hunting, and fishing with their son, Sean.

Even though Kraig had strange rules, the couple was well-known and respected in the small town. Karen volunteered her time and energy as much as possible, and the family was well-liked. Emily attended the Saint Louis College of Pharmacy, while Lauren was an honors student at Columbia High School.

From the outside, the family appeared to be living an idyllic, suburban life. However, Karen eventually called her sister Lynn and confided that their relationship was anything but ordinary behind closed doors.

Despite Kraig's ample income, he scrutinized every purchase Karen made. She was given a strict allowance for clothing, personal items, and even groceries. When Kraig arrived home from work each night, he diligently reviewed her receipts for the day.

In addition to the allowance, Kraig kept curfews. He was adamant that his wife adhere to his very specific rules. She was not allowed to have phone calls after 8:00 p.m. because 8:30 was their time for sex. Every night, without question. Karen openly told her friends of Kraig's bizarre rules. When Lynn asked what would happen if she was sick, she replied, "Well, I better be on my deathbed."

Karen's life at home was strictly regimented, with Kraig imposing timers on everything she did. She told her sister that she had always complied with Kraig's demands to maintain harmony in their marriage, but as his behavior became increasingly extreme, she felt trapped and scared.

Karen told her sister that she was desperate to find a method to escape Kraig's controlling conduct. She was seeking a way to occupy her time that he couldn't control.

Karen was looking for an outlet so badly that she joined a local gym. Kraig was okay with it as long as she did it when the children were at school and he at work, and of course, she still needed to find time to take care of the home.

Right away, Karen became obsessed with her workouts at the gym, so much so that the staff noticed her enthusiasm and offered her a job as a personal trainer. Although it represented a significant deviation from her previous career path, Karen was overjoyed with the chance and her newfound independence.

During one of her shifts at the gym, Karen crossed paths with Sunny Reese, a fellow personal trainer. The two hit it off immediately, bonding over their passion for fitness. They became fast friends and eventually scheduled all of their shifts together. From that point on, they were inseparable.

Karen and Sunny grew close, and Karen finally felt she had found someone who not only truly cared about her but also had no desire to control her. For two decades, Karen had been mentally worn down by her husband, and before long, the relationship between Karen and Sunny became romantic.

Although Kraig was aware of Karen and Sunny's friendship, Karen knew she needed to tell him the truth. She needed to tell her husband she was having an affair with a woman. To her utter shock, Kraig was okay with it. In fact, he encouraged it. He urged her and Sunny to take weekend trips together and share their time as much as possible.

Over time, he started messaging Sunny and sending her flowers, hoping he could somehow be included in their affair either as a participant or a spectator. But much to Kraig's surprise, they wanted no part in a threesome. They had a sincere connection with one another, not just a sexual fling.

———

Kraig didn't take long to realize he was being shut out. Sunny had filled a void in Karen's life that he couldn't fill. He realized they were falling in love, and his plan for a threesome had blown up in his face. Kraig had lost control of the relationship, filling him with helplessness, jealousy, and rage.

Several months into Karen's affair with Sunny, Kraig decided that moving the family away from the situation was the best course of action. He started looking for new employment possibilities to help them relocate, and he ultimately found one in Columbia, Missouri, where he became the highest-paid worker in the community. In Kraig's mind, the move would solve everything.

The Kahler family moved to Columbia in June 2008, and Kraig hoped that things would return to his twisted version of normal. He believed that putting physical distance between Karen and Sunny, who were now nearly 700 miles apart, would cause the affair to fizzle out. But that wasn't about to happen. They emailed, texted, and called each other every chance they got. Sunny spent her weekends flying to see Karen, or they would drive halfway and meet in the middle. Once again, Kraig's plan had backfired, and the two women became closer than ever before.

Still determined to put a stop to the relationship, Kraig regularly examined Karen's emails and texts and monitored her phone calls. When he found a card that Sunny had mailed her, he flew into a jealous rage.

In late 2008, Karen and Kraig received an invitation to a New Year's Eve party in Weatherford from a friend they had left behind. However, when they arrived, Kraig was surprised to find that Sunny had been invited too.

During the weeks leading up to the party, Karen and Kraig's relationship had become increasingly toxic. But after drinking a few celebratory cocktails at the party, Karen and Sunny relaxed and let their guard down. Their previously-hidden lesbian relationship was suddenly out in the open. The two women touched and caressed each other in front of Kraig and their friends. The once-secret affair had now become openly public.

Drunk, embarrassed, and enraged, Kraig stopped the party and announced to the crowd that his wife was having a lesbian affair. He screamed, "Our perfect marriage is a sham!" In response, Karen reached over to Sunny and kissed her full on the lips.

Twenty-eight days after the New Year's Eve party, Karen Kahler filed for divorce and moved into a spare room in the family home. Feeling frantic and desperate, Kraig reached out to Karen's family members, pleading with them to talk sense into her. He begged them to convince her to call off the divorce, explaining that she was having an affair with another woman and was intent on taking his money and their children. But Karen's family, of course, wholeheartedly supported her and refused to intervene.

In late February, Sunny did her best to intervene in their feud and sent a text to Kraig,

> "She's only staying with you because she believes that right now, it's best for the kids. She doesn't love you, Kraig."

But Kraig refused to believe it was over. In his mind, their life was perfect. No one could take that away from him.

The looming threat of divorce consumed Kraig's every thought, and his job suffered. At work, he carried a large binder with photos of his "perfect family," asking his co-workers, "Why would anyone want to ruin this?"

That March, during a heated argument with Karen about the divorce, Kraig became physical. It was inevitable. The day after the assault, Kraig was taken into custody outside of the City Council building where he worked, and he was charged with suspicion of assault in the third degree as his coworkers watched.

Although Kraig told police he had only tried to hug his wife, Karen told police he had violently grabbed her and left bruises on her arms,

> "Over time, it has become apparent that Kraig is controlling. I have learned along the way that he is capable of using force. The issues vary, but I figured out how to keep things from becoming ugly. When money was a problem, I wouldn't tell him what things, groceries, clothing, etc., cost. When it was about sex, I decided it was easier to give him what he wanted every night than to refuse. On occasion, I would refuse. He has been known to be forceful and mean. I'm afraid it will escalate so far that someone is going to be seriously hurt."

No matter what he did, Kraig's problems seemed to escalate. The divorce was inevitable. Karen had moved into a small house and had taken the kids with her. His two daughters had turned against him; they fully supported their mother and her new relationship. Kraig resented the rejection and bitterly referred to the girls as "rotting corpses." He stopped responding to calls or texts from his daughters, choosing only to speak to his son.

By September 2009, Kraig's anger had overcome him. His work was slipping, and he randomly left work without notice to spy on Karen. It was all he talked about, and his employer had had enough. He was asked to resign from his high-paying job, he sold his house, and at forty-eight years old, he moved in with his parents. Everything he valued in the world was gone.

Karen and Kraig were legally separated, and he was ordered to begin monthly payments of three thousand dollars in child support. Kraig was days away from a court appearance for the assault charges, and the divorce was scheduled to be finalized by January.

He became increasingly reclusive and erratic. Although he was treated for depression and prescribed anti-anxiety medication, he refused to take the drugs. Instead, he stewed in his anger and grew increasingly despondent.

———

Only ten-year-old Sean spent Thanksgiving day with his father, while the two girls spent the holiday with Sunny, Karen, and Karen's sister, Lynn. Afterward, Karen picked Sean up and took the children to visit their great-grandmother, Dorothy Wight, in Burlingame, Kansas, about 20 miles south of Topeka.

Karen, Emily, Lauren, and Sean spent the Saturday after Thanksgiving with Dorothy in her tiny, rural farmhouse. Just before 6:00 p.m., a neighbor noticed a red SUV speeding near their house. The neighbor watched as a man parked near Dorothy's farmhouse, exited the vehicle, and stomped toward the front porch. He was carrying a large object, but the neighbor couldn't quite make out what it was.

Thinking that the man might be stealing something, the neighbor grabbed a flashlight and headed outside to confront him, but the man saw he was being watched, got back in the SUV, and sped off. The neighbor called 911 to report the man, and the sheriff's office dispatched a deputy to investigate.

Moments later, however, the SUV returned and parked in Dorothy's driveway again. Kraig Kahler emerged from the driver's seat carrying a semi-automatic assault rifle. He then ran into the farmhouse and began shooting.

Eighty-nine-year-old Dorothy called 911 and screamed into the phone,

> "Help, Help! He's in the house! Somebody's coming to kill us! He's killing us! Get out!"

By the time the sheriff's deputies arrived, it was too late. The SUV was gone, and deputies rushed into the house, where they found Dorothy bleeding out on the living room floor. She had multiple gunshot wounds but was still alive.

As they searched the house, they found Karen in the dining room. She, too, had been shot twice but was already dead. Eighteen-year-old Emily had tried to hide behind a couch but had also been shot twice. She was pronounced dead at the scene.

Then a deputy heard a faint voice coming from down the hall. In a bedroom, they found Lauren, who had been shot in the chest but was still alive. She cried when asked who shot her, "Kraig, my dad."

Dorothy and Lauren were rushed to the hospital, where Dorothy also confirmed that Kraig had broken into the house in a psychotic rampage and shot them all. Sadly, Lauren was pronounced dead shortly after arriving at the hospital, while Dorothy clung to life in intensive care.

Deputies found Sean safe at a neighbor's house. The boy explained that he was cleaning old coins in the kitchen sink when he saw his father enter the house with a rifle. He reacted quickly and ran out the back door as he heard shots ring out. He then ran around the house to the front door to get to a phone, but when he heard more shots ring out, he ran to the nearest neighbor and cried for help.

After putting out a call for help in locating Kraig Kahler, the police received a report of a man who had abandoned his vehicle and was running along a country road. When officers found the vehicle, they knew it was Kraig's. Inside, they found ammunition and an unopened prescription bottle of anti-anxiety medication with Kraig's name on it. They also found a backpack filled with canned food, towels, soap, and toilet paper. However, there was no sign of Kraig.

The morning after the massacre, Kraig was found on the side of a rural road covered in dirt and with a confused look on his face. He was carrying a pistol and a hunting bag filled with pocketknives, gloves, a flashlight, and several hundred dollars in cash. When officers confronted him, he didn't resist. He simply said, "I'm the guy you're looking for."

Kraig was brought to the police station for questioning, where he lamented to detectives about his family troubles. He cried about how he had lost control of his wife to a woman, the embarrassment it caused him, and how Sunny and Karen had robbed him of his perfect life. He seemed unconcerned, however, about the lives he had taken.

Kraig Kahler was charged with first-degree murder and aggravated burglary. His bail was set at ten million dollars. On December 1, after three days in intensive care, Dorothy Wight died from her injuries.

Kraig sat in jail for the next year awaiting trial. During his preliminary trial in December 2010, he pleaded insanity, as it was the only defense against capital murder. His attorneys argued that he had suffered a mental breakdown triggered by Karen's affair, the loss of his job, and the need to move in with his parents. Everything had piled up, which had caused him to snap. They cited the unopened medication found in his car, ongoing erratic behavior, and the fact that he didn't try to conceal his actions as evidence of his unsound state of mind.

The state of Kansas enacted a law in 1995 that eliminated the conventional insanity defense. According to this new law, defendants could no longer assert that they were unable to distinguish between right and wrong due to mental health problems.

Under the new law, the legal responsibility for a crime fell upon defendants with mental health problems. However, they could not be held accountable if such problems impaired their ability to act with intent or premeditation. Kraig's lawyers contended that his mental health condition was so severe that it indicated a lack of premeditation; the crime was committed in a sudden outburst.

His attorney claimed that he suffered from depression and hallucinations during the murders. He also claimed that he exhibited traits of obsessive-compulsive, narcissistic, and histrionic personality disorders.

However, the prosecution contended that the crime was undoubtedly premeditated. His conduct over the previous year indicated that he had been building up to his ultimate objective, which was to murder his wife and potentially anyone who opposed him.

According to the prosecution's expert psychiatrist, Kraig suffered from clinical depression but could still plot the murders.

Moreover, they emphasized that Kraig had had the opportunity to kill their son, Sean, but chose to spare his life. His decision demonstrated a deliberate choice. Therefore, this was not a case of an individual who had lost control and committed the act in a moment of insanity.

The prosecution's star witness, Sean Kahler, who was now twelve, spoke via video link. Sean bravely recounted the events of the terrifying evening. Court attendees reported that Sean was persistent, articulate, and far more mature than his age.

> "When my dad entered the room, he shot my mom, and I heard her fall to the floor after the gunshot. I caught a glimpse of her, and I believe she was clutching her leg." Sean said.

The gruesome photographs of the crime scene were so disturbing that some courtroom observers had to look away, and a few were even moved to tears. The prosecution presented evidence of Kraig's numerous instances of abuse and controlling behavior, arguing that these actions reflected his longstanding intent to cause harm.

Sunny Reese also provided testimony, describing Karen and Kraig's relationship as highly abusive and expressing her desire to safeguard Karen from him. She also disclosed that Kraig had initially welcomed her and Karen's relationship and didn't seem bothered until Karen decided to leave him. However, she admitted that she lacked any tangible proof to corroborate her account, as it was based solely on her memories and what Karen had told her.

After a brief deliberation of only two hours, the jury reached a unanimous verdict on August 25th, 2011. Kraig Kahler was found guilty of capital murder, and his pleas of insanity were dismissed. As a result, he faced either life imprisonment without the possibility of parole or the death penalty.

Before the sentencing was announced, victims had a chance to read their statements. In his statement, Sean Kahler said he didn't want his father to be put to death, as it would be hard on his grandparents. He said, "I do not want my whole family to be gone."

One week later, Kraig Kahler showed no emotion, remorse, or regret as he was sentenced to death.

According to eyewitnesses present in the courtroom, Kahler instead appeared to take pride in himself, often smirking and making sarcastic comments. As he departed the courtroom, Kahler shouted to his parents,

> "Take care of Sean so he's not raised by a bunch of freaks."

In 2018, the Kansas Supreme Court upheld Kahler's death sentence, and the US Supreme Court later confirmed it in 2020. In January 2023, Kahler's attorneys filed yet another appeal, citing fourteen reasons why his conviction and death sentence should be overturned.

CHAPTER 12
THE KUWAITI WEDDING

The country of Kuwait has long been a flashpoint for conflict due to its location between the major powers of Saudi Arabia and Iraq. Nonetheless, despite its turbulent history, the small nation has been able to prosper economically, primarily because it has access to the sixth-largest oil resource in the world.

Short, moderate winters alternate with long, sweltering summers in Kuwait's hot and arid environment. From May through October, Kuwait has its peak summer temperatures, ranking among the hottest regions on the planet. Temperatures can rise above 49 degrees Celsius or 120 degrees Fahrenheit. Both humans and animals have a tough time surviving in the intense heat.

———

Nasra Yussef al-Enezi was raised in Kuwait, but little is known about her childhood beside the fact that she had mental health problems for much of her life. Nonetheless, despite the seriousness of her illness, Nasra's mental health difficulties were disregarded because of the widespread stigma associated with them in Kuwait. Nasra kept her problems private throughout her adolescence, which prevented her from receiving a diagnosis, therapy, or support, leaving her to suffer alone.

In her late teens, Nasra had a reputation for acting erratically, impulsively, and unpredictably. She nonetheless married the affluent 31-year-old Zayed Zafiri despite her suppressed rage and mental instability.

Their first son, Shaqha, was born when Nasra was eighteen, and Muhammad was born two years later. They were a wealthy family and lived relatively happily, but Nasra was burdened with overwhelming stress. Both of their sons had special needs that exceeded the norm for their age and required a high level of care and attention.

Sadly, by the time the oldest boy was five, Zayed had drifted apart from the family. He had not intended for his life to develop as it did, with him married to a woman who was constantly under the strain and demands of caring for two children with special needs. This realization fueled his selfish desire to seek an additional wife, despite its detrimental impact on the already struggling family.

Polygamy, an entrenched cultural practice in Kuwaiti society for millennia, was neither legally prohibited nor viewed as a religious taboo. It was, and still is, widely accepted for men to have up to four wives at any given time.

Amid the mounting challenges of raising two special needs children and suffering from her own mental problems, Zayed's decision to seek out a second wife was a crushing blow for Nasra. While she remained at home, devoting her time and energy to caring for their children, her husband sought a new wife. With every day that went by, her repressed anger and emotions festered inside her.

———

In traditional Kuwaiti matchmaking practices, matchmakers create profiles of potential partners and present them for consideration. Once a suitable match was found, Zayed made plans for a wedding without hesitation.

But the news that Zayed sought a second wife was like a knife through Nasra's heart. Now twenty-three, she had devoted the past five years of her life to caring for him and their children. The thought of her husband abandoning her in her time of need was too much to bear.

She believed that Zayed resented her for the disabilities their children suffered and that he was seeking a new wife in hopes of having healthier children. The thought that he could so callously discard her and their children for his own selfish desires enraged her. In late spring 2009, Zayed's decision to marry again ignited her jealousy and rage.

———

Nasra's world was shattered, and she felt like a stranger in her own home. Her once-loving husband had become distant and cold, leaving her alone to care for their children. She sat at home with her children and stewed in her anger. She was a ticking time bomb, and her mental health suffered.

———

Despite the fury and anger simmering inside her, Nasra decided to keep a level head. She refused to let her emotions get the best of her and refrained from impulsive or attention-grabbing actions. Like she had done her entire life, she hid those emotions from the rest of the world.

Although she felt a burning desire for revenge against her unfaithful husband, she was willing to bide her time and wait for the perfect opportunity to strike. As the days and weeks passed, Nasra carefully plotted her revenge.

———

As the sun beat down relentlessly on the desert sands of Kuwait, another ordinary day had begun. However, for Zayed and his new bride, August 15, 2009, was anything but ordinary. It marked the day of their highly-anticipated wedding ceremony, set to take place in Al Jahra, a city located just west of Kuwait City.

Kuwaiti weddings were renowned for their opulence and grandeur, and Zayed's nuptials were no exception. While the traditional Kuwaiti style had given way to more Westernized ceremonies in recent years, the price tag for such an event remained exorbitant. It was not uncommon for such festivities to cost hundreds of thousands or even millions of dollars, ensuring the celebration was as extravagant as possible.

Flowers imported from Holland, food sourced from Paris, and entertainers from around the world were common at these lavish affairs. For Zayed and his new bride, no expense had been spared in creating a wedding that would be the talk of the town for years to come.

The grand tents had been erected to accommodate the guests, and as the clock struck noon, the wedding festivities were well underway. The massive tents used at Kuwaiti weddings symbolize the country's rich cultural heritage and the importance placed on family and community. They are a testament to the wealth and opulence of the nation and serve as a stunning backdrop for the celebrations that take place within them.

In keeping with the tradition of Kuwaiti weddings, the men and women celebrated separately. The men celebrated in their own tent, while the women and children celebrated in another. The absence of men allowed the women to shed their head and face coverings, relax, and enjoy the festivities.

The exteriors of the massive tents were adorned with elaborate decorations, such as twinkling lights and colorful fabrics with intricate patterns that gave them an elegant, luxurious appearance.

Once inside, guests were treated to a feast for the senses. The interiors were decorated with beautiful and ornate furnishings, including plush carpets, embroidered cushions, and dazzling chandeliers, creating a warm and inviting atmosphere. The space was divided into separate sections, each designated for a specific purpose such as dining, dancing, and socializing.

The tent reserved for the women and children was grand, white, and designed to keep cool in the sweltering Kuwaiti heat. The vast structure accommodated hundreds of people and provided ample space for guests to socialize and enjoy the day's events.

However, the tents hired for this occasion were not built to typical safety standards. While they were large and spacious, they had only one exit, making them virtually inescapable in the event of an emergency.

————

While the music, food, and conversation continued to fill the air, Nasra lingered in the background, consumed by a burning desire for revenge against her husband. Her resolve had not faltered despite the passing of weeks, and she remained determined to make Zayed pay dearly for his betrayal.

Amidst the searing heat of August, the Kuwaiti desert seemed to throb with an almost palpable sense of malice. As the guests enjoyed the party inside, Nasra's maid, who was attending the wedding, observed her employer pouring liquid around the perimeter of the women's tent.

Nasra's demeanor was chilling as she poured the liquid around the perimeter of the women's tent. As the maid approached and asked what she was doing, Nasra's response was ominous. She revealed that she was enacting a dark ritual to impose revenge against her husband, using what she called "cursed water." The cursed water, however, was gasoline.

With a cold determination in her eyes, Nasra continued to douse the tent's perimeter with the highly flammable liquid, knowing that the slightest spark could ignite a devastating blaze. The scorching temperatures, which had soared to well above 122 Fahrenheit (or 50 Celsius) that day, only added to the already volatile situation.

As Nasra retreated to a safe distance, she ignited the gasoline; within seconds, flames erupted, devouring everything in their path.

Amidst the celebration and merriment, no one inside the tent had any inkling of the danger that was rapidly unfolding around them. There was no warning or acrid smell of smoke to give them a chance to run for the single exit. The flames were upon them almost immediately, and panic ensued. Women and children frantically searched for a way out, but the enormous maze of tables and chairs throughout the tent proved to be impossible obstacles to navigate amid the chaos.

Guests nearest to the door climbed over each other, clamoring for daylight. They began to push and shove, each eager to be the first to escape. However, the narrow exit could not accommodate the sheer volume of people. A stampede of panicked guests inevitably descended into a frantic frenzy, trampling one another in their haste to flee.

The sweltering Kuwaiti heat, which had already been oppressive before the fire, only fueled the flames, causing the temperature inside the tent to rise to a staggering 930 Fahrenheit or 500 Celsius.

There was simply no time for emergency crews to react. Within a mere three minutes since the first spark had ignited, the entire tent had been reduced to a smoldering pile of charred debris, with even the metal frames of furniture and clothing having been melted by the intense heat.

Sadly, amid the disorderly panic, all the guests couldn't make it out alive. Flames had engulfed the tent and claimed the lives of those who remained trapped inside. The horror of Nasra's actions became all too clear.

———

The aftermath of the tragic incident saw emergency responders sifting through the ruins of the tent, desperately searching for any signs of life. The intensity of the blaze had left many of the victims unrecognizable, adding to the already-daunting challenge of identifying them. Piecing together the identities of those lost in the inferno would be a near-impossible task.

As the chaos subsided, the harrowing aftermath of the disaster came into sharp focus. The fire had claimed the lives of 41 innocent women and children, leaving their families and friends shattered by grief and despair. Although some of the guests had managed to escape the flames, a staggering 90 people had sustained injuries in the chaos that ensued, some from burns and others from the frantic rush to flee the scene. The tragedy had left an indelible mark on the community, and the road to healing would be a long and arduous one.

To help identify the victims, a team of specialists was called in, equipped with dental and medical records to aid in the identification process. As the days passed, the situation grew even grimmer, with several of those who had been critically injured in the attack eventually succumbing to their burns.

The final death toll was nothing short of devastating, with a staggering 57 innocent lives lost and a further 74 individuals left injured and traumatized by the tragic events.

The sheer magnitude of the crime that had been committed made it one of the most devastating tragedies in the history of Kuwait, leaving the affected families and communities reeling with sorrow and anger.

Although the bride and groom had managed to escape unscathed, the focus quickly shifted to the critically-injured victims, who were being rushed to hospitals across the region for life-saving treatment.

As authorities launched their investigation into the cause of the devastating fire, initial theories centered around possible electrical faults or burning incense as a potential catalyst. However, as the investigation progressed and more evidence came to light, a much more sinister truth began to emerge. It was quickly determined that the blaze had been intentionally set as the result of a malicious act of arson.

Zayed and his new wife were both highly regarded members of their respective communities, with no known enemies. Nasra, for her part, had been largely reserved in her frustrations, and as a result, few would have suspected her of involvement in the tragedy. Nonetheless, due to her close relationship with Zayed, she was brought in for questioning as authorities attempted to unravel the events that had led to the devastating act of violence.

The community was left reeling with disbelief as they struggled to come to terms with the shocking turn of events, with many finding it almost impossible to reconcile the reality of the situation with their previously-held perceptions of those involved.

Authorities arrived at Nasra's home to interrogate her about the deadly fire, and she trembled with fear as they pressed her for answers. Finally, overcome by emotions too strong to suppress, she confessed to the heinous crime. She admitted she had doused the wedding tent with gasoline and set it ablaze. The magnitude of her actions sent shockwaves through the community, leaving them reeling in disbelief at the darkness that had been hiding beneath the surface.

Later, however, when advised to seek legal representation, Nasra's tone suddenly shifted. She adamantly denied any culpability for the crime. She formally requested the retraction of her confession, citing pressure during the interrogation as the reason for her initial admission.

Unfortunately for Nasra, her plea was ultimately denied, and her confession remained a pivotal piece of evidence throughout her trial. The course of justice had been set in motion, and the tragic consequences of her actions would reverberate throughout Kuwait for years to come.

The case's legal proceedings took several unexpected twists and turns. During her time in custody, it was discovered that Nasra was pregnant with what would have been Zayed's third child. This presented a unique challenge, as while capital punishment is legal in Kuwait for murder, pregnant women are exempt from the death penalty.

Two months later, however, Nasra was no longer pregnant and claimed that her husband had arranged for a prison guard to administer medication that caused her to miscarry. Despite the severity of her allegations, no investigation was carried out, and no medical examination was conducted to verify her claim. Nasra raised this defense during her trial in March 2010, but it did little to sway public opinion.

It is unclear whether she had truly lost her child or if it was a fabricated story to take the death penalty off the table.

In Kuwait, it's common for victims' families to give up their right to seek justice. This could mean that the accused person doesn't have to be put to death. Even though the court only needed one waiver to consider this option, none of the victims' family members chose to sign one.

Nasra's defense team did everything in their power to try and save her from the ultimate punishment, but it was a losing battle. They played on her age, gender, and mental health, but the evidence, the victims' families, and the court all stood against her.

Despite her defense team's attempts to reduce her sentence to life imprisonment, they were unsuccessful. Nasra changed her story, claiming she never intended to start the fire. She argued that she had mistaken the gasoline for water. However, the court rejected her improbable explanation.

Nasra was found guilty of murdering 57 women, seven of whom were children, and injuring 74 others. She was sentenced to death on March 30, 2010, since her alleged pregnancy could not be verified.

The court's verdict was firm, reflecting the heinous nature of her crimes. In Kuwait, only one other woman had ever been sentenced to death, making Nasra the second. Her actions left no room for mercy, and the memory of the victims and their families would never be forgotten.

On January 25, 2017, thirty-year-old Nasra Yussef Mohammed al-Enezi was executed by hanging in a private ceremony, providing some sense of closure for the victims' families. On the same day, three other women and three men were also hanged. While the media were usually allowed to attend such executions in Kuwait, they were denied access to this particular event due to a member of the royal family being among those executed. He had murdered his disabled nephew during a dispute.

————

In the aftermath of the tragedy, authorities made sweeping changes to wedding regulations, prohibiting uncertified tents and enforcing stringent safety measures. The event left a lasting scar on the peaceful nation of Kuwait, which prides itself on its low crime rates. It was unimaginable that a single person could cause so much devastation and suffering in just three minutes.

Although Nasra claimed she did not intend to kill anyone, her actions were premeditated, and 57 innocent lives were lost.

Nasra failed to kill her intended target, the bride, but the bride's mother and sister lost their lives in the attack.

Online Appendix

Visit my website for additional photos and videos pertaining to the cases in this book:

http://TrueCrimeCaseHistories.com/vol11/

More books by Jason Neal

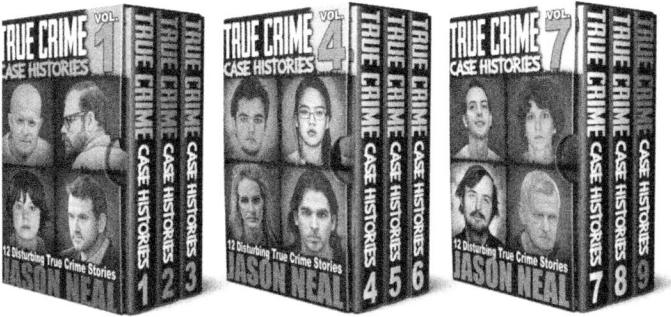

Looking for more?? I am constantly adding new volumes of True Crime Case Histories. The series **can be read in any order,** and all books are available in paperback, hardcover, and audiobook.

Check out the complete series at:

https://amazon.com/author/jason-neal

All Jason Neal books are also available in **AudioBook format at Audible.com.** Enjoy a **Free Audiobook** when you signup for a 30-Day trial using this link:

https://geni.us/AudibleTrueCrime

FREE BONUS EBOOK
FOR MY READERS

As my way of saying "Thank you" for downloading, I'm giving away a FREE True Crime e-book I think you'll enjoy.

https://TrueCrimeCaseHistories.com

Just visit the link above to let me know where to send your free book!

THANK YOU!

Thank you for reading this Volume of True Crime Case Histories. I truly hope you enjoyed it. If you did, I would be sincerely grateful if you would take a few minutes to write a review for me on Amazon using the link below.

https://geni.us/TrueCrime11

I'd also like to encourage you to sign-up for my email list for updates, discounts, and freebies on future books! I promise I'll make it worth your while with future freebies.

http://truecrimecasehistories.com

And please take a moment and follow me on Amazon.

One last thing. As I mentioned previously, many of the stories in this series were suggested to me by readers like you. I like to feature stories that many true crime fans haven't heard of, so if there's a story that you remember from the past that you haven't seen covered by other true crime sources, please send me any details you can remember, and I will do my best to research it. Or if you'd like to contact me for any other reason free to email me at:

jasonnealbooks@gmail.com

https://linktr.ee/JasonNeal

Thanks so much,

Jason Neal

ABOUT THE AUTHOR

Jason Neal is a Best-Selling American True Crime Author living in Hawaii with his Turkish-British wife. Jason started his writing career in the late eighties as a music industry publisher and wrote his first true crime collection in 2019.

As a boy growing up in the eighties just south of Seattle, Jason became interested in true crime stories after hearing the news of the Green River Killer so close to his home. Over the subsequent years, he would read everything he could get his hands on about true crime and serial killers.

As he approached 50, Jason began to assemble stories of the crimes that have fascinated him most throughout his life. He's especially obsessed by cases solved by sheer luck, amazing police work, and groundbreaking technology like early DNA cases and, more recently, reverse genealogy.

Printed in Great Britain
by Amazon